WE NEED ONE OF THESE!

Mike Evele & Doug Hepfer

with Jim Vinoski

COPYRIGHTS

First edition – January 2025

ISBN 979-8-9878413-0-3 (Paperback)

979-8-9878413-2-7 (eBook)

CONTENTS

FOREWORD

"We need one of these!"

Those words came from Duane Sheldon, who was Superintendent of Grandville Public Schools in 1998. Grandville is a very good public school in an average midwestern suburb, and those words were Duane's reaction when visiting one of the early *FIRST®* Robotics events in Michigan. Those words set in motion a chain of events that would eventually lead to the development of one of our country's finest educational robotics programs.

As head coaches of that program, the Grandville RoboDawgs, we're proud to present here the story of how it came to be. We're incredibly proud of what the hundreds of people who volunteer with our program each year have accomplished – and the unbelievable impact the program has had on tens of thousands of students. But this book isn't about bragging or blowing our own horns. We firmly believe that what Duane Sheldon said is true for every community in America. We needed a competitive robotics program, and so does your local school. Competitive robotics makes science and technology tangible for students of all ages. The self-motivation and desire to perform that only comes with competition drives students to accomplish amazing things.

We hope this book will help compel community, school, and business leaders to seek out and support their area's competitive robotics programs. In telling the RoboDawgs story, we want to share stories from our years of involvement that will encourage and invigorate our fellow coaches, volunteers, and teachers around the country as they work to further develop their own programs. Most of all, we want this story to inspire students and adult leaders in those communities that still don't have competitive robotics programs to take the leap and get them going.

We hope you enjoy this book as much as we've enjoyed the years that have provided the stories we share.

Doug Hepfer and Mike Evele, January 2025

ROBOTS IN AMERICAN POP CULTURE

The concept of a robot has been around for a very long time. Talos, a giant bronze man, was first written about by the poets Hesoid and Simonides around 700 B.C. According to the story, Talos was commissioned by Zeus and built by Hephaestus to protect the island of Crete from invaders. Talos circled the island three times every day and threw boulders at approaching enemy ships. The concept of a machine serving mankind was envisioned nearly 3,000 years ago, but we are finally living in the period when these creations of mythology and science fiction are being built in the real world.

Americans, in particular, have been increasingly fascinated by robots over the last hundred years. Arthur Daemmrich, Director of the Lemelson Center for the Study of Invention and Innovation at the Smithsonian, wrote:

> The United States has been a hotbed of innovation since its founding. From the 18th century to today, waves of immigration have brought people and ideas into close contact. The resulting cross-pollination has produced an American style of in-

novation unlike others around the world. After World War II, the United States took a global lead in public and private spending on research and development, with the government often also acting as the initial large purchaser for still-experimental inventions in electronics, telecommunications and biomedicine. At the same time, a large middle class emerged that was able to buy—and soon demanded—innovative goods and services. Over this history, a distinctive culture developed, characterized by high tolerance of failures, structural supports for intellectual property, financial backing ranging from venture capital to public stock offerings and a drive for novelty across the visual arts, music, food and technology.

Robots are a key area where society has innovated. They've been a part of our world of fiction for well over a century. The Tin Woodman showed up in L. Frank Baum's *The Wonderful Wizard of Oz* in 1900. The science fiction short story, "I, Robot" by Eando Binder was published in 1939, and it inspired Isaac Asimov to begin his more famous series of robot stories that were published as a book under the same name in 1950.

Robots turned up in movies early on, too. Interestingly, escape artist Harry Houdini made the movie with the first appearance of a robot, a 15-installment 1919 silent-movie serial called *The Master Mystery.* (It's also interesting to note that the word "robot" hadn't even been coined yet at that time. It would appear the next year, created by playwright Josef Capek.) The Tin Man appeared once again, this time in the movie version of *The Wizard of Oz* in 1939. A robot with a mean streak a mile wide showed up as the visiting alien Klaatu's sidekick, Gort, in 1951 in *The Day the Earth Stood Still.* And the wildly popular Robby the Robot made its first appearance in 1958's *The Forbidden Planet.* Perhaps the first robot that many older Americans remember is B-9, the robot in *Lost in Space.* This robot, with bellows-covered arms and legs and a glass bubble for a head, was designed by Robert Kinoshita, the same man who had designed Robby for *The Forbidden Planet.* To be brutally honest, though, those early robots weren't much to look at. They were clunky things and looked a lot like trash cans with legs.

The development of real robots was moving slowly, but robots in entertainment kept getting better. In the early 1960s TV cartoon *The Jetsons*, the title family's household chores were well taken care of by the humanoid robot Rosie. Then, in the 1970s, we saw a veritable cascade of more advanced cinematic automatons, with that decade featuring the original *Star Wars* with R2-D2 and C-3PO, along with The Gunslinger and all the other 'bots of *Westworld* and *Future World.* The 1980s gave us the title characters of *The Terminator* and *RoboCop*, along with Johnny 5 in *Short Circuit.* From the 1990s on, there are too many movie robots in too many forms even to keep count. There were all the different ones in *The Terminator* franchise and the Fembots in *Austin Powers: International Man of Mystery.*

If there was one period which represented the coming of age for robots in popular culture, it was the period from 2004 through 2014. In this period, many modern robot concepts were developed and evolved. *iRobot*, released in 2004 and starring Will Smith, looked forward to the year 2035 (not that far off) when highly intelligent robots filled public-service roles and evolved to conspire to enslave the human race.

The animated picture *Robots*, released in 2005, depicted a world of sentient robots where a striving young inventor named Rodney (voiced by Ewan McGregor) disrupted an evil plan to make all robots submit to forced upgrades. The next big animated robot movie, *WALL-E*, came in 2008, right on the heels of *Robots*. This movie is charming and unique for its lack of dialogue. There are only 17 lines of dialogue in the entirety of this one hour and thirty-eight minute movie. The storyline revolves around the last robot remaining on earth, WALL-E, who spends his days tidying up the planet. One day he spots EVE, a shapely probe sent back to Earth on a scanning mission. WALL-E embarks on his greatest adventure when he follows Eve across the galaxy.

The coming of age for robots in movies continued with *Real Steel*, released in 2011. It stars Hugh Jackman as Charlie Henton, a prize fighter robbed of a future when towering robots take over the boxing ring. Charlie teams with his estranged son to piece together scrap metal to build a championship fighting robot. Then we have the release of *Pacific Rim* in 2013, an action film where a washed-up ex-pilot (Charlie Hunnan) saves mankind in its battle with ancient sea creatures.

The following year saw a pair of blockbusters with robots as central characters. Disney released its first animated feature from the Marvel Comics series, *Big Hero 6*, in 2014. This movie tells the story of a young robotics prodigy who upgrades his late brother's healthcare-provider robot to defeat the masked villain who was responsible for his brother's death. This movie was a popular hit, and it won an Academy Award for Best Animated Feature. One more 2014 movie rounds out this ten-year burst of robot movies – *Ex Machina*. Starring Oscar Isaac, Alicia Vikandee, and Domhall

Gleeson, this movie focuses on the evolution of a humanoid robot with artificial intelligence. The Turing test is a central plot element, as a young programmer tries to determine if the humanoid robot is capable of exhibiting intelligent behavior indistinguishable from that of a human.

In just ten years, these seven movies had thrust robots deeper into popular culture. Featuring big-name stars and Hollywood-size budgets, these movies have expanded our concept of robots and given them a more central role in our future.

Let's talk about actual robots! In 1994, adults started the first robotics competitions. Marc Thorpe, a designer for Lucasfilm, created the robot combat sport Robot Wars, in which remote-controlled robots fought to disable each other in an arena. Thorpe held four annual events around the U.S. from 1994 to 1997. The concept was picked up for television. The first version of the British television series *Robot Wars*, featuring both professional and amateur robot operators using remote-controlled robots to "fight to the death" in a glass-and-steel arena, ran from 1998 to 2004.

Adults continued to compete with robots in the entertainment arena. The reality series *BattleBots* originated on Comedy Central and ran for five seasons, until 2002. After being mothballed for over a decade, it was picked up by ABC and ran for seven seasons there. It was later picked up for a short run by the Discovery Channel. *BattleBots* thrilled audiences with three-minute competitions featuring a variety of robots of different shapes and sizes, all remote-controlled, competing to destroy their opponents. This real robot competition evolved to become primarily a Las Vegas show, playing popular robots daily in a scripted show. Think WWE for geeks.

The UK's *Robot Wars* television series also made a brief reappearance on the BBC, from 2016 to 2018.

Over the last fifty years, all these robots in the fictional realm made the machines "real" to most Americans – long before the needed technology caught up and brought them into genuine existence.

THE EVOLUTION OF ROBOTS AND COMPETITIVE ROBOTICS

In the real world, meanwhile, robots were also capturing imaginations, but in a very different way. They were mostly built by engineers to perform basic, repetitive tasks in manufacturing settings. Automation in industry began in the 1960s, starting with very simple pick-and-place tasks, but soon began moving on to more advanced jobs such as spot-welding. Industrial robots made their debut as mass-production machines in the 1970s, and really started to take off in the 1980s. They soon proved their capabilities in taking on the most hazardous and difficult jobs in the industrial world. Most of the early such robots were static machines with safety fences and interlocks to protect the people around them. However, there were also automated guided vehicles (AGVs), which first appeared in the 1950s as simple tow trucks that followed wired paths to move things around in warehouses and factories. Eventually, that technology would merge with the more advanced robotics automation and create true autonomous mobile robots (AMRs) that perform a variety of tasks.

While none of these machines were a hit in pop culture, they represented a confluence of critical importance: the marrying of all the popular markers from the decades of fictional portrayals of robots with the fast-evolving technology that was finally making real-world robotics possible.

> **Mike:** Doug, when you and I were in high school, competitive robotics couldn't have happened. The technology wasn't there and the computing power wasn't there. Advances in our ability to manufacture components and to create faster processors and computers has allowed our kids to build and compete with robots. Engineering advances have allowed us to deal with small scales so readily. We can work with sizes of things on the order of light wavelengths now. We can build microchips very precisely and cheaply to the point where this technology is available to ordinary people. Now kids can use it to build robots and play these games because the technology has advanced to that degree.

> **Doug:** From my perspective, we've moved from robots we saw in movies and on TV to things kids can build because there have been significant developments with regard to the types of parts and processors we could use with students. You mentioned miniaturization. When I went to college, the first computer I worked on filled a room the size of a high school gymnasium. You have said that you remember, when you left high school, there was a room that had some Apple IIe computers in it. Computers were big, bulky, and didn't have a lot of computing power in today's terms. If you look at what's happened with that today, we have microprocessors on our robots which weigh

just ounces and have more computing power than anything we just talked about in the past.

Mike: That made a transition possible – from robots that our imaginations created, like the *Lost in Space* robot – to real robots designed and built by students.

Doug: We had this miniaturization take place, but also we had new technologies. Think about global positioning system (GPS). When we were young, if you wanted to find your way, you needed to find a compass and look for the stars...

Mike: And a good map.

Doug: ...and a good map, because without a topographic map and a good compass, you were lost. Today, all of our drones use GPS to navigate. Even some of our land–based robots use GPS to navigate. These robots receive signals from seven or more satellites. They fix a location within a matter of inches. Then the kids can use that technology to create this autonomous unit that will go accomplish something. Look at camera technology. When I was a kid, the Polaroid SX–70 was a big deal. You could push a button and see a picture in just moments. Today, our robots have these Intel cameras with two lenses that use parallax to measure distance. They can track 100 colored blobs in the field of vision of the camera and tell the processor how big they are, where they are located in three dimensions, and help a processor prioritize attacking those game elements based on information from the camera. From push a button and watch it develop while you shake the photo to a camera that actually provides this wealth of data – and it's a $300 camera. There are so many instances where technology matured, sizes came down, and the cost came down radically.

Mike: There you go. Manufacturing, computing power, and price have all gone in the right direction to make this technology ubiquitous.

Doug: If you look at LEDs, even ten years ago, LEDs were super expensive. Look where they are today. Look what the cost is of any of our robot components. Shoot. We have 3D gyros on our VEX robots that cost less than $100. When we bought the first 3D gyros for our aerial drones ten years ago, those cost more than $1,000 each. There has been such a change in the cost and availability of components. Progress like this has made it possible for robotics to move from a concept, from entertainment, to the real world. This chapter is going to look at how robots developed in the real world and then get into educational competitive robotics.

One of the key endeavors that drove advancements in the technology that supports our robots was space exploration. Continued advancement of technology that put us on the moon almost 60 years ago gave our country other new opportunities to use robots. Space exploration drove incredible advancements in robotics.

In January 2004, the *Spirit* and *Opportunity* rovers landed on the surface of Mars. Their twin 90-day missions were to analyze a range of rocks and soils to look for clues to past water activity on the Martian surface. The rovers landed on opposite sides of the planet, both in sites that appeared to have been affected by water activity in the past. They would last far beyond their planned mission durations. *Spirit* finally concluded its mission in 2010, while *Opportunity* would last all the way until 2018, when a planet-wide dust storm coated its solar collectors. *Opportunity* set a record in distance traveled by a rover, covering more than a marathon's worth of ground.

In 2012, the *Curiosity* rover landed on Mars. It was the largest and most technologically capable rover that was ever sent there. In its ten years of service, the car-size rover used its seven-foot-long arm to manipulate various tools to take rock, soil, and air samples, which it analyzed on site. It sent over a million raw images of the planet's surface back to us here on Earth.

NASA's Mars 2020 mission saw the *Perseverance* rover begin its exploration of the planet. Upon its landing there in February 2021, it set about searching for signs of ancient life and taking rock and regolith samples for potential pickup for return to Earth by a future mission. *Perseverance* also got some aerial robotic help from the Mars helicopter *Ingenuity*. After hitching a ride to the surface of the planet attached to the belly of the *Perseverance*, the solar-powered *Ingenuity* embarked on a series of demonstration and operational flights to give scientists new perspectives on Martian terrain and geology, and to help pave the way for future robotic aerial scouts.

It wasn't just Mars missions and space exploration that were getting in on the robot craze. Not long after the turn of the century, our own households started to mimic the cartoon home of the Jetsons, albeit in a less humanoid way.

In 2002, iRobot released its Roomba floor-vacuuming robot. It followed that act in 2005 with its Scooba robotic mop, and in 2006, it launched its Dirt Dog shop-sweeping robot. The following year, it launched the Verro pool-cleaning robot and the Looj gutter-cleaning robot. Meanwhile, although autonomous mowers had been around since the MowBot was patented in 1969, Bosch launched a robotic mower, Indego, in 2012 that could follow a pre-programmed pattern. And in 2020, Husqvarna announced its EPOS mower, which used satellite navigation to guide itself around your lawn.

The industrial world, too, continued the march of robotic progress. Robotic palletizers, which stack cartons of products on pallets for shipping, became a standard piece of equipment for a variety of manufacturing operations. Robot welders and assemblers made huge strides in the automotive and heavy-machinery industries. Collaborative industrial robots, specifically designed to work in close proximity with human workers, began to proliferate. These more refined automated machines are built with integrated safeguards for the humans around them, allowing them to "escape" the safety cages that surrounded the less-advanced industrial robots of old.

Who hasn't seen the Boston Dynamics robotics creations, the most popular being Spot, the agile dog-looking robot that stars in so many adorable videos? Don't let the cute videos fool you, however – Spot is a proven robotic workhorse. These dogs have played roles helping with inspections and reliability for manufacturers, sensing and data capture for power and utilities, and progress monitoring and safeguarding worker health and safety in construction, to name just a few applications.

Robots have started popping up everywhere over the

last five years. Nobody is really surprised to see a robot wandering the aisles of a local supermarket. Marty, a grocery store robot made by Badger Technologies, is designed to alert shoppers to hazards like spills. Marty is on the job in Stop & Shop and Giant stores. Tally, produced by Simbe Robotics, is used to monitor the shelves of Family Fare, Giant Eagle, and a multitude of other stores. Tally follows a designated path around the store and alerts workers to items that are out of stock and to other product presentation problems.

Recently, robots have even been showing up as servers in restaurants, bringing your food to your table. They enhance safety by patrolling airports and shopping malls. They've appeared in health care, too. Robotic surgery is now common, carried out by surgical robots with robotic arms and tiny instruments at their tips. They have specialized 3D cameras that provide the human surgeon with high-resolution images of the work at a surgical console, from which the surgeon controls both the robotic arms and the camera. Robots are also beginning to help restore mobility to people who've suffered strokes or spinal-cord injuries. ReWalk Robotics, for example, makes powered exo-skeletons and exo-suits that offer both temporary rehabilitation assistance and long-term powered hip and knee motion.

More and more, robots are becoming commonplace in the real world around us.

> **Doug:** We've been talking about robots in popular culture and robots evolving in the real world, but let's shift and talk about robots in a competitive sense. When we talk about a robot, what is a competitive robot?
>
> **Mike:** There are three tiers, or classes, of compet-

itive robots. The first tier of competitive robotics involves robots that are controlled remotely. A student has a controller with joysticks and buttons. There's some kind of radio interaction, and the robot performs across the arena under student control. Whatever the student does with the joysticks or buttons he or she is using, that's what the robot does. A good example of a Tier 1 robot would be those in the *FIRST®* Robotics Competitions (FRC®). Even though there is a brief autonomous period at the beginning of each match, the bulk of the competition is completed with the student in total control of the robot. If the robot has to pick up a cone or a cube, it's the student making those decisions and sending that command to the robot in real time.

Doug: The second tier of competitive robotics involves robots that execute pre-programmed commands. This robot is no longer under immediate student control. It has programming that a student has written, and it competes autonomously using that programming. I guess the first example I can think of would be the NXT robot from LEGO®. (The NXT replaced LEGO's first-generation Robotics Invention System.) In 2006, we used to run LEGO Saturdays in Grandville. These LEGO Saturdays were in elementary gyms, and we used them to get kids excited about LEGO robotics. In that competition, every robot had to perform autonomously. We didn't allow Tier 1 robots, which were under student control, to participate. Elementary students actually had to build and program robots, which had to autonomously carry out their instructions to win the game. In those days, it was not uncommon to have a challenge in which a robot was designed and programmed to pick up marbles and run a maze, getting over or under things in its path. The robot would then drop off marbles in three locations along the way and cross a finish line. Students would build and program a robot on a Saturday morning, and then compete on Saturday afternoon. The competition would be timed, and the combination of speed and marble handling would determine who won. Students worked to have their robots deliver all the marbles in the right place, and to finish in the shortest time.

Doug: School competitions reached Tier 3 in the last few years. These robots do more than follow a linear program written by a student – they can actually operate with some true autonomy. VEX AI was groundbreaking in the competitive robotics space. VEX AI was introduced by Innovation First right during COVID, and we competed for the first time in 2021. VEX AI competitions require a team to bring two fully autonomous robots they have designed and programmed. These two robots play as a team, against two robots built and programmed by the opposing team. There were very few competitions in that first year. I remember we won a regional competition in Texas and ended up being the Texas Champions. Our team went on to become the World Champions, winning at a championship venue that would not allow spectators due to COVID rules at the time. There was no human interaction with these robots once they were on the field. The robots were turned on, they started executing a game strategy, interacted with scoring elements, and made decisions about their next action based on sensory input. That third tier of robotics is where we are today. I see VEX AI and Bell Advanced Vertical Robotics (an aerial-drone competition sponsored by Bell) at the pinnacle of complexity of what a student robot is today.

Mike: Yes. We're getting closer and closer to what we imagined a robot to be. Robots that can make their own decisions, responding to data that is input and data they collect. In other words, robots that can "think" for themselves.

Doug: We see some of those robots in our homes today. There are some pretty smart household vacuums out there that will avoid running over the cat, that will learn the layout of the house, and that will spend more time on problem areas that are extra dirty. There is intelligence in those devices, but when we talk about competitive robotics, our kids have the ability to build and program things with that level of autonomy before they ever leave high school.

Mike: It's a matter of technology and programming, and our kids are just crossing that line now.

Doug: Let's see what the next few years bring.

With robots making the jump from science fiction to being

integral players in our industrial and retail worlds, it was inevitable that they would also become part of our educational institutions. Actually making that leap happen, though, took just the right guy. The intersection of all the robotics dreams of the past with new technologies of our time captured a true visionary's imagination. Dean Kamen, a serial entrepreneur who invented and patented an insulin pump, and then built a company (AutoSyringe) to manufacture and market it, saw a growing need for more, and better, technical education for young people. Kamen would go on to invent the iBot self-balancing, multi-terrain mobility device, the Segway scooter, and the Slingshot, a water purifier based on a modified Stirling engine that runs on almost any combustible fuel. He obviously had a good idea where the technology was headed. He knew we would need a much bigger source of skilled workers and true innovators – people who could design, build, and program cool stuff, just like he was doing.

"What I think needs to be highlighted is how little the message has changed over the years," said Kamen. "People show me a video of myself saying in 1989 that this country would fall behind in technology. I said let's embrace what works: kids love sports. The world of sports is very engaging and exciting, but there are a lot more lottery winners than pro athletes. Let's get kids, parents, teachers, and corporations together in a positive celebration of technology." Dean Kamen founded *FIRST* Robotics to get such a celebration of technology started.

FIRST Robotics

It began rather modestly. In 1992, 28 teams met for the inaugural *FIRST* event in a high school gym. By 1995, the *FIRST*

Championship was being held at EPCOT in Disney World. In 1998, *FIRST* teamed up with LEGO to create a junior robotics program, which drew 200 teams for its pilot. In 2004, that partnership expanded and launched the *FIRST*® LEGO® League Jr. – now known as FIRST® LEGO® League Explore (FLLE) – which serves children ages six to ten.

> **Doug:** We love *FIRST* because no one individual – or two, or three – can successfully build and compete with an FRC robot. These machines and their programming are complicated, and it takes a team to compete and win. Nothing that happens in a classroom during the day forces kids to work together like *FIRST* does. No sports team brings together the passion, teamwork – and brainpower – that an FRC team does. A winning FRC team has all the interpersonal and team dynamics of a championship basketball or football team, but FRC teams also require massive amounts of knowledge about drivetrains, electronics, pneumatics, sensors, cameras, and control systems. Dean Kamen was ahead of his time in coming up with all of this, and his approach was similar to Wayne Gretzky's idea of "skating to where the puck is going." He did something very different, and it worked.

FIRST Robotics was the grandfather of all educational robotics. It defined what early robotics competitions involving school-age children could look like. *FIRST* has expanded to offer programs for children and youth from ages 4 to 18, including the following:

- *FIRST*® Robotics Competition (grades 9–12, ages 14–18)

- *FIRST*® Tech Challenge (grades 7–12, ages 12–18)
- *FIRST*® LEGO® League (grades pre-K–8, ages 4–16)
- *FIRST*® LEGO® League Discover (pre-K–1, ages 4–6)
- *FIRST*® LEGO® League Explore (grades 2–4, ages 6–10)
- *FIRST*® LEGO® League Challenge (grades 4–8, ages 9–16, though these vary by country)

VEX Robotics

Soon after FRC got going, more players were getting into the academic robotics game. The largest competitive robotics program in the world today, VEX Robotics, was started in 2007 by Tony Norman, an electrical engineer, and Bob Mimlitch, a mechanical engineer. This program, which is today's leader in competitive educational robotics, was born from a *FIRST* team.

Bob and Tony were mentors for Team 148, a *FIRST* Robotics Competition team, in 1992. They competed that very first year in the inaugural FRC event and both are still involved with Team 148 today. They are among the most experienced educational robotics professionals in the industry. As engineers, they loved *FIRST*, and they saw students learn tremendous things in the early years of *FIRST* Robotics. By the mid-1990s, however, the two began to ask questions. They began to wonder, "Can't we inspire more kids? Could we create a program for everyone, not just teams sponsored by companies with deep pockets?"

At the very end of the 20th century, a large retail organization, RadioShack, partnered with Tony and Bob's new company, Innovation First, to begin to develop VEX Robotics. VEX Robotics was created following the principles that students shouldn't pay to play, that educational robotics should be available to everyone, and that coaches shouldn't be allowed to build the robot. Bob Mimlitch made this comparison: "Think of a basketball team – what would it be like if high school basketball teams allowed dads to play on the team?"

> **Doug:** It's interesting that *FIRST* Robotics really opened the door for educational competitions. *FIRST*, with Dean Kamen at the helm, blazed a new trail and said, "Let's give students a chance to compete with robots." That was the inception of competitive educational robots, but the concepts that Tony and Bob developed as they started VEX Robotics really brought forward some points that have been critical to the development of more enhanced educational robotics. The three principles they focused on are just so important to our program and to programs like ours.

> **Mike:** Yes. I think the fact VEX Robotics believed that students should not have to pay to play was a key change. The cost of doing *FIRST* Robotics for some programs is immense. The cost to run each of our *FIRST* Robotics teams is more than $40,000 per team. To support that, you need to develop sponsors who can make contributions of that magnitude. With VEX Robotics, however, you can start a team for a few hundred bucks. If I were an educator, alone, starting a robotics program, VEX really provides a bigger bang for your buck when it comes to getting robotics in the hands of your students.

> **Doug:** That first concept, that kids shouldn't have to pay to play, was revolutionary, Mike. How about

the second one: the idea that educational robotics should be available to everyone? You shouldn't have to have a fleet of engineers to lead robotics teams.

Mike: VEX Robotics created a system, a set of parts, and a set of designs that students and teachers can understand, so you don't need a cadre of engineers in the room to help you build a robot.

Doug: This was revolutionary because, with *FIRST*, where it all began, a large mentor group is necessary to be really successful with an FRC team. You needed engineers to support the design and build of a custom robot. VEX's concept that robotics should be available to everyone, and that you shouldn't need a cadre of engineers to run a team, opened this up to public schools all over the country who didn't have engineers hanging out every day.

Mike: Sure. Not every school is sitting right next to General Motors, Motorola, or NASA. VEX is more accessible. VEX is something that teachers and students can do without feeling overwhelmed.

Doug: The third principle that they address also aligns really well with our experience in educational robotics. Mike, what are your thoughts on the concept that coaches shouldn't be allowed to play? That they shouldn't build, they shouldn't write the programming, and they shouldn't operate the robot? It was a revolutionary idea when Tony and Bob laid down this principle. *FIRST* had launched competitive robotics for students and then these guys came along and changed the game.

Mike: Competitive robotics started out as something that was really complex, and it was felt that students couldn't build the robot themselves. They needed a mentor next to them, building for them, and *FIRST* was developed to inspire young people. It was meant to highlight technology, what technology can do, and how engineers contribute to the world around us. *FIRST* Robotics was created to celebrate engineering – and engineers. The principals VEX Robotics introduced made them very student-centered. Their Student Centered policies prohibit coaches, moms, and dads from working on the robot. Students need to solve the problems, doing the engineering, figuring out what they need their robot to do, and how they are going to build a robot to do it. The focus became education, whereas the focus before was inspiration: "Let's see what we could do together." It became educational in that students started realizing that what they were getting in the classroom was now showing up in real life; that they could build a robot based on their own knowledge and experience.

Doug: Essentially, you made a comment that reminded me of a transition that has been taking place over time. When *FIRST* started, the then-current technology probably did require a broad group of engineers and mentors. The technology wasn't at a cost or a level of complexity or maturity where you could expect students to master it – and so it required that mentor base. It's interesting that, as Tony and Bob made their mark in educational robotics, they took advantage of advances in technology to shift us away from the early model to one which is much more focused on the education of students.

Mike: Bringing the cost of robotics materials down also allowed teams to get smaller. You can have a team of three or four students design, build, program, test, and compete with a VEX robot. As you always say, there's no place for a kid to hide. Every student has to be involved in the project and no one student can complete the entire robot.

This radically different vision for competitive robotics proved to be very attractive to educators across America. Innovation First, the company formed to make VEX Robotics parts, had philosophical beliefs that supported education: that teams should boil down lots of ideas, that they should engage in radical creativity, and then move on to build a robot. Innovation should come first. Innovation First was unusual in that it hired most of its employees from the ranks of graduates of *FIRST* Robotics. They found that those graduates were radically ahead of their peers in the workforce because of the experience they had building a robot as a team in high school. VEX Robotics has been tremendously successful and has grown to be the largest program in the world because they have been focused on access and equity. The program's leaders have concentrated on creating a level playing field, where kids don't have to pay to play. They have created a program that is accessible to the more than 40% of U.S. schools that are Title 1 schools.

Along with VEX Robotics and Innovation First, Tony and Bob helped found the Robotics Education & Competition

Foundation (REC). The REC global mission is to provide every educator with competition, education, and workforce-readiness programs to increase student engagement in science, technology, engineering, math, and computer science. The REC created an ecosystem where the primary focus is on being a student-centered program, where adults are restricted to coaching roles and cannot design, build, or program the robot. We believe that VEX has been tremendously successful because of their focus on principles and philosophies, which align well with the factors that have driven the growth in the Grandville Robotics programs.

> **Mike:** There's something else special about VEX Robotics. In VEX, you start to build a robot, and three weeks later, you begin to compete in a league. We love the league structure, which allows teams to compete, improve, see other teams improve, compete again, and cycle through this repetitive build and test cycle centered around that league organization. One of the outcomes we see is a continual evolution of the robot. The design gets better and better with time. As students compete and see what other robots can do, and recognize the shortcomings of their own robot, their robot gets better and better. The VEX core values are "Bold Creativity," "Iteration," and "Quality." Those come through in their competitions, which we love.

"There's not a one-size-fits-all solution for robotics," said Dan Mantz, CEO of the REC Foundation, a non-profit that provides team and event support for VEX. "My daughter spent four years on a *FIRST* team. But that was in a very affluent district. Our program is student-centered. Our model works really well in rural, underserved communities. We have the largest robotics competition in the world, VEX Worlds, every April. In 2023 we had over 3,000 teams, and Quinlan, Texas, one of the poorest Texas districts, were division finalists."

Mike: We have spent the last few pages recognizing the innovations that VEX Robotics brought to competitive robotics. Lest the reader be left with the impression that VEX Robotics is better than *FIRST* Robotics, let me set the record straight. These two program both have amazing strengths and both have had a major impact on hundreds of thousands of students. But the two programs are different, and we love them both for what they are.

Doug: *FIRST* Robotics is engineering and design on a big scale. Every robot is a custom product, and students design and make unique parts to support their game strategy each year. It takes a larger team of students – we believe the right number is fourteen – to build and compete with a *FIRST* robot. This scale teaches students about organization and teamwork on a very different level than we see in the teams of three to four students who compete on a VEX team.

Mike: Our very first team, in 1998, was our *FIRST* Robotics team 288. We added teams 216 and 244 in 2009 and 2010, respectively, making us one of very few high schools in the world that fields three *FIRST* Robotics teams. We love *FIRST* for the unique things it teaches our students, and I really can't picture the RoboDawgs without *FIRST*.

FIRST was first, and who knows how long it would have taken for students to become involved with competitive robotics if Dean Kamen had not built his organization and blazed a trail? VEX Robotics (and the REC Foundation) came along and created competitive educational robotics at scale. REC Foundation programs serve more students and hold more competitive robotics events than any other organization in the world. In April 2018, VEX Robotics Competition was named the largest robotics competition in the world by Guinness World Records.

    FIRST Robotics and VEX Robotics are the two "big dogs" in competitive educational robotics, but there are many other very exciting options for students.

Other Educational Robotics Competitions:

BEST Robotics

BEST Robotics (the name is an acronym for "Boosting Engineering, Science and Technology") was also started by a pair of engineers, Ted Mahler and Steve Marum, who both worked for Texas Instruments (TI) at the time. In 1993, they were helping as guides at an Engineering Day event at their company location in Sherman, Texas, when they joined a group of high school students watching a video of freshmen at the Massachusetts Institute of Technology building a robot for one of their classes. The students expressed an interest in doing the same thing, so with the support of TI's management, Mahler and Marum established North Texas

BEST. They held their first competition that same year, with 221 students from 14 schools competing, including one team from San Antonio. That group would later establish its own non-profit group to support a local competition, and North Texas BEST mentored them. San Antonio would host its first competition in 1994, establishing the hub system of local and regional organization that BEST uses to this day.

Several more BEST hubs were established in 1995, kicking off a pace of growth that would continue for the next several years. In 1997, the group would establish itself as a 501(c)3 non-profit corporation in the state of Texas, BEST Robotics, Inc. The next decade or so saw the organization add new hubs throughout Texas and into neighboring states and beyond. In 2001, TI hosted the first BEST New Hub Workshop, and the growth through new hubs exploded.

In 2009, BEST Robotics kicked off its biennial BEST National Conference, a summer gathering for volunteers and teachers, hosting workshops on subjects such as hub execution, technology, technical training, and design. By 2010, BEST boasted 741 teams in 38 hubs, and that same year, the program held its inaugural BEST National Championship.

Botball

Still more new programs would join the mix of competitive robotics programs over the years. Botball Robotics, aimed at middle school and high school students, got its start in 1997. It was launched by the KISS Institute for Practical Robotics (KIPR), a non-profit that was established in 1995 by Cathryne Stein, Dr. David Miller, and Dr. Marc Slack, with the mission to spearhead technology and science education programs based on robotics. KIPR held the first Botball national competition in 2001, and the first international participant joined in 2003.

Botball seasons run from January to May. Students begin by attending a workshop to learn computer programming, and they then have six to eight weeks to design, build, program, and test their robots. Teams must document their progress along the way, and record any changes they make during that time. They then compete, first at the regional level, then moving on to national and international competitions.

We fielded Botball teams from Grandville Middle School from 2007–2009. We really liked the creative technology that KIPR introduced, and our middle school teams did very well against high school and college teams. We moved on from Botball as VEX Robotics systems came into widespread use.

MATE Underwater Rovers

The Marine Advanced Technology Education (MATE) Center was established with funding by the National Science Foundation via a grant to Monterey Peninsula College in 1997. The MATE Competition Network began in 2001 and currently consists of 46 regional events that take place across the U.S. and around the world. Regional competitions serve as feeders into the annual MATE World Championship.

MATE's mission is to inspire and challenge students to learn and creatively apply STEM skills to solving real-world problems in a way that challenges their critical thinking, collaboration, entrepreneurship, and innovation – and prepares them for the Blue Economy workforce.

Bell AVR

The Bell Advanced Vertical Robotics (AVR) Competition was started in 2019 to inspire future entrepreneurs in the fields of engineering and manufacturing. Students use hands-on, industry-standard tools to design, build, and compete against teams from around the U.S. with the most advanced aerial robotics technology available today. Participation in the Bell AVR Competition prepares students to meet rapidly changing future workforce needs, both on the ground and in the air!

For the first three years, Bell AVR events were held only in Texas. In their fourth year, 2023, the competition expanded to include a Great Lakes Region, centered in Michigan.

VEX AI

In 2020, VEX Robotics released VEX AI, the most advanced technology in competitive robotics. This new competition is the only one that exists entirely within the third tier of competitive robotics. The robots use a Game Positioning System to sense its location on the field. Advanced cameras and sensors determine the position of game pieces and other robots. The programming allows the robot to make decisions based on incoming data. This is an amazing leap forward and, frankly, everyone is still trying to figure it out.

> **Doug:** We have focused this chapter on educational robotics competitions because competition is one of the critical reasons these extra-curricular teams add so much to a student's school experience. The pressure of competing on the field, and the limitations imposed by time, forge learning and accomplishment at a different level than any other learning environment. Robotics competitions,

though, are quite different from other types of competitions that students engage in.

What is a robotics competition like and why are they so different from athletic competitions?

Participating in, or being a spectator at, an educational robotics competition is quite different from being involved with an athletic competition. There are three key differences between most robotics competitions and traditional athletic competitions.

1. **Alliances:** Most robotics competitions create environments where students must work with students on other teams. In most competitions, teams work together in alliances to defeat their opponents. In FRC, it's a Blue Alliance of three teams against a Red Alliance of three teams. In VEX, it's a Blue Alliance of two teams against a Red Alliance of two teams.

2. **Cooperation:** The principles of good sportsmanship are built into the rules for competitive robotics. This concept is so important that MIT professor Woody Flowers went so far, in the context of *FIRST*, to coin the term "Cooperatition" for cooperative competition. In many *FIRST* games, there is an element of collaboration between the two opposing alliances built into the game. This sounds strange at first, but there is often a link in the scoring in which something that helps your opponent helps you as well.

3. **Gracious Professionalism:** This is an often used term that is sometimes misinterpreted. It is not uncommon in competitive robotics to see teams helping each other

to build and program their robots. You would think that, in the cutthroat world of competition, the last thing you would see is teams helping other teams. If you saw a robot that is in poor shape and a team struggling to get it working, that would be an advantage to your team because you will easily beat them in the next match. *In robotics, the opposite is true.* We constantly observe teams helping other teams. We lift each other up, and by doing so, we make each other better and the overall competition better. Our teams have helped numerous teams and we have been helped in return. We have had so many amazing competitive experiences. The pressure of time and competition with other highly capable teams really brings out the best in our students.

Mike: In March of 2013, we were on our way to a tournament in Toronto. Because of other student commitments and other time pressures, we left Grandville in three groups at three different times. Among our vehicle caravans, we had two trailers, one containing the three robots and most of our tools and another carrying the students' luggage, spare parts, and the rest of our tools. As my vehicle was entering the Toronto area, I got a call from Doug saying that one of our trailers from an earlier travel group was missing and presumed stolen. My first reaction was complete disbelief. How could we be missing a trailer? As we drove on, the facts became more clear. Our trailer with the lead group (the one with the luggage and spare parts) was being towed by a parent followed by a coach with a group of team members. They had made it to the hotel and had gone inside to check in. When they came back out, 20 minutes later, the trailer and the truck that had been towing it were gone. Stolen. We were able to send the third travel group, who were on their way but still in Michigan, back to Grandville to get extra clothes and toiletries for the students who lost their luggage – but our spare parts, our computers, and a significant number of our tools were gone. We made it to our competition with our robots, but we were without everything lost in the trailer.

Doug: What happened next was amazing! It seemed that every team at the tournament came to us with tools, gift cards, and offers of help with our robots and programming. It was like the tournament hugged us. "Gracious Professionalism" is more than a fancy term. It's the culture of caring and doing what is right. It was remarkable what good can come of such an awful incident.

THE EARLY YEARS:
1998 TO 2007

The RoboDawgs story begins, as most stories do, with one person who passionately believed that Grandville Public Schools needed a competitive robotics team. This happened at a time when no one in Grandville had heard of such a thing, and the future of competitive robotics was unclear at best.

Doug: When you look at the Grandville Robotics program, you have to look at the inflection points that occurred in our history. It's hard to understand 26 years without looking at the key events that shaped us. There have been seven key moments that have defined our program. At each inflection point, there were decisions made and the program moved in a new direction. We could have crashed and burned at any of those points, but instead, our program has been fortunate. Each one of those inflection points generated positive momentum that helped us evolve into the program we are today. If I think about those seven key points in time, the first one was obviously when the program started.

Mike: Our story starts with a local engineer, Natalie Lowell, who discovers this new competition called *FIRST* Robotics at an SME conference. She becomes enamored with *FIRST* and decides that our local high school needs to build and compete in the *FIRST* Robotics Competition. That was the beginning of our program. Natalie ran with this idea, negotiating with both X-Rite and with our school administration to begin the process of starting a team. Our superintendent came to me and another teacher, Spencer Dolloff, and we started the program.

Doug: Our first inflection point was an SME conference in 1998 and the passion it raised in a local engineer.

Mike: [chuckles] That's right.

The story of our robotics team begins with a young engineer newly employed at local company called X-Rite. Natalie Lowell first learned about *FIRST* Robotics at a meeting of the Society of Manufacturing Engineers. She went on to attend a *FIRST* Robotics Competition at Eastern Michigan University and was amazed. If you have never attended an FRC event, you should. It is nothing like you would imagine a robotics competition would be. The atmosphere created by the lights, music, and announcing puts these events on par with rock concerts. Alliances of robots compete against each other and, in between matches, students dance on the sidelines and cheer on their teams. The pit areas are alive with activity as teams of students, mentors, and engineers tinker with their 125-pound robots in preparation for their upcoming matches. These events are celebrations of what students can do with their minds and hands. For Natalie, it was like nothing she had experienced before. She had walked into a place where those with ability in science, technology, engineering, and math were lauded as loudly as those with ability in sports are in the rest of the world.

Natalie immediately saw the truth of Dean Kamen's often quoted saying that "FRC is the only sport in which everyone can go pro!" She left the FRC competition excited and filled with the resolve that she would start a *FIRST* robotics team. If public education was to remain relevant and fit the needs of both students and companies in need of people with the skills and passion to become engineers, students everywhere would need an opportunity like this.

Her first job was to sell this idea to the CEO of X-Rite. She knew that, in order start a team, she would need to change not just the culture of public education, but also the culture of a multinational corporation. She would need the help of engineers as well as educators. To accomplish her goal, X-rite would need to open its doors to students and teachers – an unheard-of concept in 1998. With tentative approval from X-Rite, she approached the nearest school district, Grandville Public Schools.

It was at this time that Duane Sheldon, who was then Superintendent of Schools for Grandville, got his first look at an FRC. That's when he uttered that immortal line that became the title of this book: "We need one of these!" Those five simple words would eventually change the trajectory of the lives of thousands of kids in Grandville and beyond.

He didn't wait around either. Duane had always been very much his own person, and he had strong ideas of what education should be. He had always pushed innovative ideas in our high school and in our libraries. It was his strong support that saw the Grandville robotics program get off the ground.

> **Doug:** You'll see a theme develop here. From Duane Sheldon forward, this program has always enjoyed amazing support from Grandville superintendents who have shared a strong vision for the future.

Duane conscripted teachers Spencer Dolloff and Mike Evele, along with Natalie Lowell, to start his high school robotics team. They had the unconditional support of the administration – and no idea what they were doing. They, in turn, recruited a small group of some of their best students, and invaded the closed world of corporate culture and engineering secrets that was common back in 1998.

While recruitment of RoboDawgs is quite open today, students were handpicked for that very first year. RoboDawgs today come from a true cross-section of the student body with a wide variety of interests and academic abilities.

Very early on, the RoboDawgs were the beneficiaries of a group of very innovative people at X-Rite, who took the team under its wing. X-Rite was founded by a group of seven engineers at aircraft instrument maker, Lear Siegler, Inc. who wanted to form a new company as a sideline. This innovative spirit made them a great partner for a new *FIRST* Robotics team. X-Rite's first product, X-ray marking tape, had been introduced in 1968 and was the basis for the company's name. The company moved beyond its highly successful first product to introduce a densitometer for photographic printing use in 1975. The company went public in

1986 and, in 1987, they had moved into a new headquarters and production facility in Grandville, Michigan. X-Rite had some great engineering knowledge and talent, including individuals like Larry Lowell (Natalie's husband), Tim Gates (from *FIRST* Robotics team B.O.B. in Zeeland), Terry Stevens (from Rockwell Automation), and Dan Deprekel (Head of R&D at X-Rite), among others. These people gave of their time and expertise to help our students learn, grow, and become excited about engineering and technology. The extremely talented professionals at X-Rite provided their patience and tremendous amounts time to support our students, giving the fledging team a chance.

In the early days, the RoboDawgs all ended up working long hours at X-Rite – pretty much every night during the *FIRST* "build season." A new *FIRST* Robotics game is announced the first week of January, and the infamous "build season" runs from then until a "ship date" in late February. This created many weeks of long days with very late nights, and our team often worked from 3:00 p.m. to 11:00 p.m. during this period. The company had several engineers who worked with the team every night.

The RoboDawgs attended their first competition at Disney World's Epcot in Florida, and that experience cemented the early path for our young team. Natalie Lowell and the team at X-Rite would go on to support the team for many years.

We learned early on just how demanding the schedule for a *FIRST* Robotics team can be. After weeks of long hours after school, Mike was unable to attend the Florida event because his first child was born around the same time. He had worked throughout the season with the team. He had set up the flights and helped the team prepare to compete, but he wound up staying home for the arrival of his first daughter. Mike missed that first competition and, with the responsibilities of his new family, he found he just couldn't continue to put in the long hours required by the team. Mike stepped down as a RoboDawgs coach, but he continued to see the great impact participation in the team had on students. He didn't know it yet, but he'd be back as a head coach a decade later.

For the next two years – the 1999–2000 and 2000–2001 school years, Scott Joseph, an assistant principal at the high school, became head coach of the team. He kept the team going through these early years.

Mike continued to be involved with after-school science, taking on a coaching role for Grandville's Science Olympiad team. That's where he would first meet Doug Hepfer. He and his wife Rosemary were actively supporting activities their children were involved with, including Science Olympiad for the middle school, LEGO League for the elementary school, and Scouting. Along the way, they learned that there were threads common to successful programs. They formed the Grandville Academic Team Boosters to support academic teams in Grandville. That organization was formed to help develop strategy and actively advocate for academic teams, to support those teams through coaching-staff recruiting and development and to help them develop improved materials and methods. They educated parents and the public, publicizing the activities and accomplishments of Grandville academic teams. The group made sure the focus of programs was on students, not on the adults who ran them. They were committed to programs that would expose team members to real-life applications of science and mathematics and conducted fundraising to provide supplemental financial assistance to competitive academic teams.

When Doug's daughter moved up to the high school, Mike was running Grandville's High School Science Olympiad team. Doug offered to help with the team, and a relationship began which would have great implications for Grandville's robotics program down the road.

Meanwhile, as Mike was taking what turned out to be a detour through Science Olympiad, the RoboDawgs team continued under the care of Natalie and the team at X-Rite. The team continued to grow and prosper in those early years, but change would come six years later.

> **Doug:** The team was off to a strong start with X-Rite, but then, six years later, the RoboDawgs reached their second inflection point.

> **Mike:** Yes. Natalie Lowell left X-Rite in 2004, and the team lost that strong support from the company. A Grandville High School teacher, Ron Denning, was the coach at the time and discovered suddenly that he had very few mentors engineers to help the students. The team went through a significant change as the students had to do everything. There were team parents who worked at companies that allowed the team to make their custom parts, but the students now designed and built everything. And they had a banner year that year. It was a major change in the program as they moved away from a "mentor inspiration" type program to become more of an educational program.

> **Doug:** Wow. First inflection point, we launched.

Second inflection point, we have a major course change to become more student-centered. The coach at the time realized that there was tremendous value in having students do all the designing, building, and programming of the robot – and that they can be successful doing that.

From the 2001–2006, Ron Denning was the RoboDawgs' head coach. Ron's tenure saw two major changes to the team.

First, many of the engineers that helped in the early years left X-Rite to pursue other jobs or moved on to help other *FIRST* teams. Dan Deprekel of X-Rite was there to offer his help, but there was much less support from the professional engineers at X-Rite. As a result, the culture of the team shifted from a model in which students were apprenticed to an engineer who worked side-by-side with the student to a model that was entirely student-centered. There were no more adult hands on the robot. Students did everything from design to part fabrication to the building and testing of the robot. This is something that has become a bedrock principle of our program.

Second, the RoboDawgs began to spawn and mentor new robotics teams in the surrounding communities. The Wyoming, Michigan robotics team began during this time, and the RoboDawgs were key mentors for this new team. Ron gave up some of the RoboDawgs' sponsors to help fund the Wyoming team and other fledgling teams. This is something that has remained in the DNA of the program. The RoboDawgs continue to start and sponsor new robotics programs in West Michigan, around the US, and in Canada.

Doug: The third inflection point shows up just a year after Natalie Lowell left in 2005. A few Grandville parents and teachers had become very involved with another young *FIRST* program, *FIRST* LEGO League. We had LEGO League teams at a couple of our elementary schools, and four parents decided we needed more of these. They thought we needed a structure to support LEGO League teams at our elementary schools. They put a program in place to develop teams across all of Grandville's elementary schools. In short order, they had not only developed teams at all of those schools, but they also held the first Grandville regional LEGO League competition.

Grandville had its first regional LEGO League competition in 2005. Four individuals, including Doug, drove the activity that year. Tom Chicklon (you'll see his name later in the book) is currently an FRC coach, but Tom got his start as part of the group that built the program to support LEGO teams at all our schools. Chuck Parks was a tremendous asset as we built this program. He started coaching LEGO League in 2004 and supported LEGO teams all the way through 2015. He was also instrumental in so many new things the high school teams did with technology. Rosemary Hepfer, Doug's wife, began coaching LEGO robotics in 2005. She still runs our elementary programs today, supporting LEGO League and VEX IQ teams at all our elementary schools. This core group – Tom and Chuck and Rosemary and Doug – laid the foundation for a program that would support LEGO League teams in all our schools. This was a significant shift from "team" thinking to "program" thinking, and it helped us build a feeder program to develop stronger robotics teams as kids advanced through their years in school.

Ron Denning left the RoboDawgs team in 2006, and a group of parents took the reins and continued the team. Dan Hall, Jeffrey Nelson, and Ken Orzechowski, among others kept the team alive through a time without an educator on the coaching staff. Their own kids were going through the program at the time and these coaches kept the opportunity available for both their own and other students at Grandville High School. The RoboDawgs team continued in these years, but another inflection point was coming.

In 2008, there was a major coaching change as new superintendent Ron Caniff decided that an overhaul of the team was necessary. He has a vision for a program that would sustain itself, pass on knowledge from one year to the next, and grow in both the number of students involved and types of robotics offered. This is where Doug and Mike enter the picture…

Doug: As the RoboDawgs moved toward the close of their early years, it was clear there were two important things had been going on in parallel during those years.

Mike: On the high school side, we started the team in 1998–1999 school year. I left the team for ten years, and in the intervening years, the team went through five changes of leadership. The team had some good years and learned along the way.

Doug: The RoboDawgs went through quite a transition over that first decade, but in parallel to that, from 2004 forward, another group in Grandville was building a program to support LEGO League teams. While the FRC team was learning about how to be an FRC team and building its skills, the LEGO League teams were turning into a program. That really provided a foundation for the overall robotics program when those two came together.

SETTING THE FOUNDATION: 2008-2014

In 2008, the team was poised for yet another change. Circumstances convinced the district administration that the team needed to be rebuilt from the ground up. The focus and mission of the team needed to change, and a new direction meant new leadership. Grandville's Superintendent of Schools at the time, Ron Caniff, declared a go/no go situation: either new leadership would take over the RoboDawgs, or he'd shut the team down. Ron reached out to Doug. Doug went to Mike. Bringing Mike and Doug's combined experience, with the support of Rosemary Hepfer, Tom Chicklon, and Chuck Parks, had the potential to make the RoboDawgs program unique and successful at a whole new level. Doug and Mike agreed to take over the coaching duties for the RoboDawgs that year.

Before they did, however, they asked themselves, "If we're going to take on this team, what do we think is important?" They wrote a document of operational guidelines, sometimes referred humorously between them as their manifesto, in which they mapped the five priorities that they thought should be central to the new organization. They said to themselves, "This should be an educational program." They laid out expectations around grade standards and around the structure of the revamped RoboDawgs. They specified that this would be a year-round program and thought about how that should be structured from a coaching standpoint. They concluded that the right structure was to have two co-head coaches – a coach who was a parent and a coach who was an educator. Finally, they lobbied the Grandville School Board to give them full authority to run the program according to those principles.

> **Mike:** I think the fourth inflection point occurred when you and I came on the scene at the high school level. It started when you came in one day and said, "How would you like to build some robots?" I gave it some thought overnight and I came back the next day saying, "Yes, let's do this." This was the beginning of a sea change in our program. It was a complete change in direction. The principles we introduced in 2008 changed the team's direction in a major way. We chose to begin thinking of Grandville Robotics as a program, rather than a temporary collection of teams, parent coaches, and students. This program thinking also changed the paradigm that the RoboDawgs was just a *FIRST* Robotics team. We began to look at *FIRST* Robotics as just one part of what we did to engage students with hands-on science and technology. This program thinking was the first major shift called for in our manifesto.

> **Doug:** You and I became co-head coaches in 2008 and we have run the program ever since. We put all of our robotics programs under one umbrella.

The elementary programs, the middle school programs, and the high school programs shifted to operate under the RoboDawgs umbrella and follow the principles in the manifesto. One new principle that stemmed from making the RoboDawgs a year-round program was the shift in focus to encompass a variety of competitive robotics programs in addition to FIRST. We began to build out middle school robotics as the bridge between our elementary LEGO teams and our high school teams. The teams became academically focused. We transformed Grandville Robotics into an educational program, and, as a result, high school students must now meet certain grade requirements to participate in the team. We implemented more stringent grade requirements than any other team I could think of, and we put in place the means for students to achieve those goals. We instituted a dedicated robotics study hall. These changes in 2008 have supported our RoboDawgs in meeting the grade standards ever since. This shift to being an academic program was the second major change introduced in the manifesto.

The manifesto set the tone for an educational robotics program. It was the first time the district had considered a program approach to robotics, and it was endorsed by the school board, the principals, and the superintendent. We will share more about the manifesto in a later chapter as we describe the five major operating principles supporting our robotics program.

As the team transitioned to new leadership, two important mentors became part of the high school coaching staff.

Tom Chicklon followed his son up from LEGO League in the lower grades to *FIRST* Robotics in the high school. He mentored the team all four years that his son was a part of the team. Tom immediately embraced the philosophy of a student-centered model that keeps coaches' hands off the robot and puts students at the forefront of building and discovery. Tom is not a professional educator, but is still a true teacher. He has tremendous patience, kindness, and technical knowhow. Tom really loves the students. In fact, after his son graduated from high school, he stayed with us and is an indispensable part of the program to this day.

Chuck Parks also joined Mike and Doug's new coaching group. Chuck had been instrumental in the development of the Grandville LEGO League program and jumped right in to help with the RoboDawgs. To call Chuck a wildly creative engineer would be an understatement. Chuck was an electrical engineer with a passion for kids and a heart of gold. Having Chuck put an inspirational engineer in a leadership role, but he firmly believed that kids should do all the work. His sons came through the RoboDawgs program, but Chuck stayed on for many years after they graduated. Chuck remains involved with the Grandville Academic Team Boosters today.

The stage had been set for the fifth inflection point to come in five years. It was big! First, let's cover the five years leading up to that big change.

In 2008, the RoboDawgs had traveled to the national championship and placed last among FRC teams. But the two new head coaches believed that, by sticking to the principles they had outlined in their manifesto, the team would turn things around. A core belief of this new coaching group was that every student should be hands-on with the robot. So, ten years after the RoboDawgs were founded, Grandville High School added a second FRC team, Team 216 – "More RoboDawgs."

The 2009 season started with the teams working out of a mechanics garage in the basement of the district administration building. That venue became too small for the growing team so they rented an unused retail space – a former vacuum-cleaner repair shop – in a strip mall in Grandville. This new home of the RoboDawgs had some advantages and disadvantages, but they finally had a dedicated space to build their robots.

The team spent many long evenings in that new space, and the students had meals during long build nights from the Subway across the street or the Chinese restaurant next door. The team became very familiar with the menus of both establishments! The retail space was a godsend, yet it was less than ideal. The team created a practice field in an area with incessant roof leaks and there was some very nasty-looking mold growing above the ceiling tiles. There was only one electrical outlet in the space – and it was in the bathroom. So the bandsaw was located in the bathroom that year!

Our first *FIRST* tournament was in Traverse City that year.

Doug: We went to play in Traverse City and, of course, being new coaches, we were very concerned that our robots had some shortcomings.

Mike: We were quite convinced that we weren't going to do well compared with the other robots

– not just because the coaches were new to this, but because almost all the students were also new to the team.

Doug: That first year, we weren't sure what parts we needed, or where to get them. Like many first-year teams, we went to our first event scared that we were going to embarrass ourselves. Then we got to the field and our first match started. There were six robots on the playing field that morning – and nobody moved. That competition, called Lunacy, was played on a slippery surface covered with bathroom wall panels. The robots had special, slippery plastic wheels and every movement on the field created static electricity. Our biggest issues at Traverse City had nothing to do with our robot's design or construction – we burned out several sets of electronics at that event because of the static electricity.

Mike: We walked into the event feeling we didn't know what we were doing. The learning curve was extremely steep. Many of the robots at that first tournament had the same problems that ours did. We were actually in much better shape than we thought we would be. We proved something that has become part of our accumulated experience – showing up is half the battle. After their first tournament, the kids immediately knew what they wanted to do for the next one. They came home and decided to rebuild one of the robots.

Doug: Our second event was at Grand Valley State University a week later. We came home and one of the teams (Team 216) said, "Oh my gosh, we see some things we'd like to adapt." They decided to tear the top half off the robot off and rebuild it. Being new coaches, we were terrified by the idea that a team would scrap something that had taken five weeks to build and replace it in five days. (We have learned over the years, by the way, that radical rebuilding happens often and typically results in great innovation and accomplishment.)

Mike: We took a cautious approach that week in 2009, telling the kids to keep the old robot component together and to be prepared to put it back on the robot if they were not done with their upgrade by Thursday night. They took the top half of the robot off and went to work. From Sunday through Thursday night, they accomplished more than they had in the previous five weeks. They totally rebuilt the top of the robot.

Doug: They were motivated to do well. They realized in the first tournament that it was all about throughput. They wanted to pick up and process as many balls as possible. We went to Grand Valley to play and, astonishingly, this robot that had been in the bottom third of the robots in Traverse City won the Grand Valley event. It was our first win with us as coaches. For the kids, it was just a mountaintop high.

Mike: It was. It just ignited their self-confidence. They felt that they could do this crazy game. We learned a ton about what the kids need – how to set short-term goals for them, for example, because students will tend to build everything at the last minute. We slowly started to get a handle on what parts we needed to order, what supplies we needed, and how to support the students as they explored this process of building and modifying their robots.

Doug and Mike's first full year running the program was a success. The RoboDawgs won the Xerox Creativity Award at the Lansing FRC competition. The team's alliance were champions at Grand Valley State University FRC tournament. The RoboDawgs were on their way.

After the success of 2009, the following year, the district gave the team its first dedicated space in a former cafeteria of what is now an administration building. One corner of the space was transformed into a machine shop, and most of the remaining space was used to create an FRC practice field.

In the fall of 2010, the RoboDawgs established their own autonomous boat challenge, in part to help fill in a gap in the robotics program year. This was before Grandville began participating in the VEX Robotics program, and their FRC-only format left a good portion of the year open. (VEX would later help make the program officially a year-round one.)

> **Doug:** We're fresh into 2010 and jumping into a new season. We decided to purchase a number of remote-control boats, add autonomous capabilities, and have an autonomous boat race. We were going to race boats in the Grand River. It was a grand idea, no pun intended. We bought these

boats from a foreign country. They were a pretty good size, but we had to make all the electronics ourselves. At the time, you just didn't have devices designed to provide autonomous control of a craft. We actually built electronics with the help of Custom Electronic Products, which was Chuck Parks' Company. He made our electronics that first year. Mike, I'll never forget testing them in the high school pool. It was our first outing, we were full of excitement, and we put them in the pool, and then...

Mike: Yes. We put them in the pool and the kids are tooling them around, first controlling them using remote controls. Suddenly, there's a loud bang like a gunshot. Everybody looked around – we didn't know what was going on. Where did that sound come from? We continued running the boats. Then it happened again. This huge sound just blew us away. We grabbed one of the boats and we opened it up and we realized that the capacitors were not rated for the voltage we were putting across them. Basically, the insides vaporized and blew out the casings on the capacitors. It was a small explosion going off in each one of those boats as it was tooling around the pool!

Doug: It was fun because that capacitor was part of the original equipment we bought from the boat manufacturer. The power we were putting through it was coming through the board we had made. We learned a lot about mating our equipment with other people's equipment that first year.

Boats gave our students their first experiences with autonomous craft, and with a very dynamic hardware and software environment. Every year, the technology in our boats changed, so the kids had to acquire a fresh understanding each time. They then had to write new code every time. Eventually, they were writing autopilot code to handle wind and currents. Groups of kids would write parts of the code, and the next group would come in and pick up from there. The boats had the students doing Agile development before Agile was even much of a thing. The challenges they ran into included things like figuring out the code to go from a heading of 359 degrees to a heading of 1 degree without going all the way back around – introducing yet another set of real-world math and programming challenges.

> **Doug:** We started building boats to get more out there for the kids to do. But it was also the desire to go to space that led us there. We developed our own technology for autonomous boats. We built boats no one else in the country was building. With all the learning we had about the hardware and programming we used to build them, the boats became the father of the drones the team is building now.
>
> While we're talking about boats, we're going to have to talk about that very first boat race, the Great American River Race in the Grand River. We had this brilliant idea that we were going to race these boats (that were about 30 inches long) on the Grand River. Now, not being frequent boaters on the Grand River, we really did not understand what we were getting into.

Mike: [chuckles]

Doug: There were some things we didn't understand.

Mike: That's right. For one thing, it was really, really cold in a river in Michigan in November.

Doug: For another, there's a lot of stuff floating in that river that you don't expect.

Mike: Not just leaves, either.

Doug: Old tires, refrigerators…

Mike: [laughs] Yes. There was so much floating in the Grand River we never thought about.

Doug: Well, in that first boat race, none of the boats completed the race. In fact, fishermen brought two of them back to us as they hit things or got stuck along the way. Our first race in the Grand River was a dismal failure. We had a great time on a freezing-cold day in the fall, but not one boat crossed the finish line, and we never again raced in the Grand River.

In the fall of 2010, our new cafeteria space provided room for each team to build its FRC robot!

This was also the year that we began to play in additional FRC events outside the state of Michigan. Michigan had moved to a District structure for FRC competitions with the idea that every team could play two local events. We believed that our teams – playing student-designed, student-built robots – needed to play more than twice a season. Robots designed by professional engineers perform well right out of the box, at the first event. Robots designed by students often have issues that need to be worked out over the first couple of outings. During our first season, we had learned a lot about the difference between teams like us and teams that play robots that are designed and built by professional engineers.

We started the 2010 season playing at a regional event in Milwaukee, Wisconsin. Our teams had a tough time with the game that year, and we had shipped one of our "robots" to Milwaukee with just a frame and wheels. Our kids basically built that robot in their pit in Milwaukee. We continued to learn so much…

> **Doug:** That Milwaukee event was one of the only times I have put my hands on a tool at an event in the last sixteen years. Do you remember that?
>
> **Mike:** How can I forget. The kids had taken that robot to inspection four times, and it was still out of size by about one eighth of an inch. They had been back and forth to inspection with that same size variance for more than an hour. We were due on the field in ten minutes. You picked up a giant mallet and said, "Hey, Mike, stand on this robot."
>
> **Doug:** Yup. We had the robot on its side, and I beat that thing into square in about ten seconds. It passed inspection right away, and went to the field to play. We told the team that, if they ever built a robot to exactly the allowable dimensions again, we would take it to the parking lot and run over it with the car.

Our teams moved on from the Wisconsin event to play at Grand Valley and Troy, where Team 288 was part of the

Finalist alliance. After the rough start in Wisconsin, we played much better, and team 288 qualified for the State of Michigan Championship in Ypsilanti. Team 288 moved on that year to play at the *FIRST* Championship in Atlanta.

In 2011, we started the season with our autonomous boat race. Learning from the prior year, we ran this race on the lakes at Millennium Park. With a second-generation boat and a year of experience behind us, almost all our teams finished the race.

The FRC season found us with a larger team, and we started our third FRC team. Adding Team 244, "RoboDawgs 3D," made us one of the only schools in the world with three FRC teams. We started our competition season in Wisconsin again that year, followed by the event at Grand Valley State University.

Our teams competed in Canada for the first time in 2011, attending the tournament at Waterloo University. We loved this event, and learned that most Canadian schools shared our belief that robots should be student-designed, student-built, student-programmed, and student-operated. The professors from Waterloo that ran the event were amazing, taking time to talk with our kids and share ideas with them. Our experience at Waterloo left us convinced that our teams should go north of the border to compete every year.

We finished our 2011 season with an FRC event in Troy.

Our year began with autonomous boats again in the fall of 2011. We upgraded our equipment and used the Traxxas Spartan hull as our base. This boat was fast, and our electronics finally reached the point where we could really race under autonomous control. That year, spectators lined the shore and docks at Millennium Park for our October race.

The RoboDawgs started their VEX Robotics program in

the fall of 2011. There really weren't VEX events in Michigan yet, so we built robots to play "Gateway" and competed against ourselves. In December of 2011, our teams competed in the first Evil iPad Challenge, working to achieve high scores that would qualify them for fun prizes.

Our FRC season in the winter of 2012 was one for the record books. That season, the RoboDawgs started handing out mementos that would become legendary: their Dawg-Tags. The first one was a small stainless-steel tag with a colored RoboDawgs logo. The designs would wind up changing year to year, but the purpose was the same – to have a small handout for all the people the teams interacted with so they would remember them. (That summer, a RoboDawgs DawgTag even traveled aboard a NASA rocket, reaching an altitude of more than 135 kilometers.)

The 2012 FRC season featured all the drama of abject failure and unexpected success. That was the year one of our teams – Team 244 – decided to build their first swerve drive.

We "competed" first in Baltimore that year, where none of our teams had a great event. We were building bumpers and writing software at night in our hotel rooms. Team 244 got off to a tough start at that event, foreshadowing struggles they would have throughout their first two events. In Baltimore, before the competition even started, some cute girls came by our pits. A couple of guys on Team 244 decided to show off and demonstrate how far their robot, which used a modified lacrosse racquet, could throw a basketball. They cranked the air pressure up in their pneumatic system, and when they went to throw the ball, the robot snapped the racquet in half. To add insult to injury, Team 244's swerve drive did not work properly at any point during the Baltimore competition. That robot spent most of its time in the pit upside down, wheels in the air, as they worked to fix their code so that unplanned rotations of the wheels did not rip the wire out of each drive motor every time they turned.

After the Baltimore experience, Team 244 had a second heart-breaking event at Grand Valley State University. The swerve-drive software they had written used encoders to sense what direction each wheel was facing. Those encoders had kept coming loose and rotating at the event in Baltimore. The team decided to fix the problem by using LOC-TITE® to help keep the encoder screws tight, but – somehow they dripped red LOCTITE all through the right rear wheel assembly as they secured the encoder screw. The result – the right rear wheel never turned at any time during the GVSU event. This team, which had finished 30th out of 65 teams in Baltimore, ended up ranked 38th out of 40 teams at Grand Valley.

Team 244 had hit rock bottom. They spent the Sunday after the GVSU outdoors in a parking lot, in the snow, solving their encoder problems and fixing their swerve-drive code. There was urgency in the air because the team was headed off to play in Waterloo that Wednesday.

Everything changed for the team in Waterloo.

With their swerve-drive code working, the 244 robot actually drove in competition for the first time that Thursday in Waterloo. On the flat, level field, they could collect and score basketballs with speed and precision. But now that the swerve drive worked, they discovered a new issue that would keep them from winning an event. During the end game, robots had to drive onto an elevated teeter-totter. Every time Team 244 tried to drive up onto the ramp, their main circuit breaker blew. You will read more about the miraculous rebuild the team completed that Friday in

Chapter 9.

Following Team 244's gearbox rebuild in Waterloo, they won every match and went on to finish second as finalists at that Waterloo Regional. This team's perseverance carried forward, and they won their next event the following week in Troy, Michigan.

Team 244's Cinderella season culminated with an outstanding performance at the *FIRST* Championship in St. Louis. The team played to an 8–1 record in the Curie Division, marking our best finish ever at a *FIRST* Championship. Then the fifth inflection point came in the spring 2012. Due to the team's success during the FRC season, and a presentation that the students made to the board of education, the school district gave the team a new home.

The program took a huge step forward when it moved into what would become the district's robotics center for more than a decade. The new space, formerly known as the Orion building, had been built jointly by Grandville and two neighboring school systems years before to house an educational program for special-needs students.

Eventually, due to budget constraints, that program was discontinued. The Grandville schools paid to acquire sole ownership of the building, but it ended up sitting vacant for two years (with the exception of being used to house track-and-field sporting equipment).

Mike: We had a really good team that year. We went to nationals and made it to the finals, reaching the highest place we had ever achieved, at sixth overall. When we came back, we did a presentation to the school board about the program, and several parents spoke about what robotics had done for their kids. Some of the presentations were very moving. A week later, Superintendent Ron Caniff called and offered us the Orion Building. That had a major impact on our program. It changed how we felt about our teams and the perception of the program in the community. Our robotics program was named as a "Point of Pride" for the school district – a distinction we still hold today. We had gone from being housed in some strip-mall space to the basement of the old Administration Building to now having our very own building with twelve classrooms and the space to try new things. That a was huge boost to the program.

Doug: This building and this jump into new space gave us credibility and greatly enhanced our fundraising ability. Donors looked at us differently when we had a big sign out in front of a school building that said, "This is the Grandville Robotics and Engineering Center." That group of students in 2012 inspired us all. That group qualified more teams for the state VEX championship than we'd ever qualified in the past. They played our FRC robot all the way to the sixth seed in one of the divisions of the FRC World Championship that year. It was a highly accomplished group that moved us into a brand-new building, and 2012 marked the fifth inflection point for our program.

Our team spent the summer of 2012 moving into the new Grandville Robotics and Engineering Center. As you will see below, this move really opened up new doors for us.

We enjoyed our final autonomous boat season in the fall

of 2012. We continued to us the Traxxas Spartan hull as our base. We had gotten much more proficient with autonomous boats over the years, and in 2013, we would graduate from autonomous boats to aerial drones.

November 2012 saw the students run their first Crowdrise funding campaign. They wanted to buy a Tormach CNC (computer numeric control) mill, a shop machine that automatically performs a set of programmed instructions to create a metal part. The RoboDawgs successfully raised the $28,000 price tag. That very same month, the team made its first parts, a set of mounts for an experimental crab-drive unit.

Following the autonomous boat race, our RoboDawg teams moved on to their first full VEX season, playing "Sack Attack." We had our second annual Evil iPad Challenge. We had our first VEX League, and held our first VEX tournament in January 2013, and qualified our first three teams for the 2014 State Championship and our first RoboDawgs teams for a VEX World Championship. Setting a precedent early, however, we did not take a team to the World Championship because we did not feel they would perform to an acceptable standard.

The 2013 FRC season was special for a few different reasons. We were in the new Robotics and Engineering Center, giving us lots of space to build and test our robots. Thanks to crowdfunding, we had new CNC machining capabilities. And during this time, the RoboDawgs also began helping new teams in Canada venture into the world of educational robotics. Students were able to mentor the Canadian students through a Polycom telepresence system. It was basically a Zoom call, in which a group of our students would talk with a group of their students. Each week, we would have a Polycom conference to discuss robot design and building in attempt to solve problems for both teams.

Our team had developed a competence with pneumatics and helped solve one Canadian team's difficulties by shipping a full set of pneumatic cylinders and other parts to Canada. Our teams then walked the Canadian team through the process of setting up and using those pneumatic parts on their robot – all over the Polycom link.

During other video conferences, the teams ventured into the philosophy of robotics. A member of one of the all-male Canadian teams, noticing that there were many young women on our side of the call, asked the question, "Why would a girl ever do robotics?" Doug and Mike stepped back because we had smart, strong, and confident young women who proceeded to put this young man in his place. One of them asked, "Why would *a boy* ever do robotics? Wouldn't it be the same reason a girl would do robotics? Girls have all of the intellectual and mechanical abilities that any boy has. In fact, our girls are probably better than your boys!" Wow. The boys on the other end of the conference stepped back from the screen. It was one of the team's favorite memories. The day a 5'0" young woman stood up for all young women of robotics and science!

RoboDawgs FRC competitions in 2013 included a *FIRST* event in Traverse City. We competed next in East Toronto, where our trailer was stolen. Our teams returned to compete in Troy, Michigan. Then we traveled to compete at the first Western Canadian FRC Regional where we would meet the Canadian teams we had been mentoring. There are many great stories from this event – read about Herman and his robot in Chapter 9.

In the spring of 2013, the RoboDawgs began building

high-altitude balloons, strapping GoPro® cameras to them and installing GPS trackers as well. In June, some of the earliest launches resulted in photos from 125,000 feet up. Three RoboDawg teams launched payloads attached to 1,200-gram weather balloons. The three capsules, all launched at the same time, returned to Earth in very different places. Team Alpha recovered their payload in Marshall, Michigan. Team Omega's capsule parachuted back to the ground in northern Ohio. Team Beta's payload, taking a fairly unusual course, landed in New Liberty, Iowa, where a very kind gentleman saw to it that the team got it back.

> **Mike:** All right. We purchased some large weather balloons and tanks of helium, and then let our students research the types of capsules you attach to one of these balloons. Our students came up with the idea to put payloads in styrofoam coolers to keep the electronics from getting too cold at high altitudes. We were using GPS trackers used by hikers. Three RoboDawgs teams made capsules, and we launched all three simultaneously from a schoolyard in Jenison. The idea is that the balloons, filled with helium will take our payloads to high altitudes where the lower pressure will cause the balloons to expand to the point of popping. A parachute then allows the payload to land relatively gently. What's strange is the three balloons must have burst at different altitudes or something because all three of them ended up in totally different spots. We had one go up, pop, and land in a cornfield around the Ohio-Michigan border. We had another capsule that landed closer

to home, by municipal airport in Battle Creek. The third just disappeared after launch. We could not figure out where it went or where it landed – until it hit the ground and the impact knocked aluminum foil off the GPS tracker in Iowa. Apparently, the students on that team, worried about the cold, decided to wrap the GPS tracker in aluminum foil. It turns out that, when you wrap a GPS tracker in aluminum foil, it cannot communicate with any satellites.

Doug: The funny thing about the capsule that landed in New Liberty, Iowa: we lost track of it for three days. Upon landing, the cooler cracked open and somehow dislodged the satellite tracker from the aluminum foil and we got a signal. Lo and behold, the third balloon had not gone to Ohio, had not landed in Michigan, but, indeed, had landed in New Liberty, Iowa. It's an interesting story because, over the years, we've launched dozens of high-altitude balloons and we've only lost one. We only failed to recover one. It landed in the middle of Lake Michigan. We were tracking all the way, it came down, the parachute didn't open, and it dropped itself, smacked up, in Lake Michigan.

Mike: At over 90 miles per hour, we figure...

Doug: The one that landed near Liberty, Iowa, came down on its parachute. It was a typical recovery process for us. Once a balloon lands, we stop and say, "Who might we know in the area?" And the answer for New Liberty was – no one.

Mike: No one.

Doug: When you land something in rural Iowa, what do you do? You call the veterinarian. I grew up in a small farm town and the vet knew everyone. So we called the veterinarian in New Liberty, Iowa, and this kind woman answered her phone. I explained that we were trying to recover a research balloon that our high school had put up. She was fairly busy that day. She had a number of animals to deal with, but she knew that that her friend, Ernie, who ran the local tavern, didn't go to work until six o'clock and perhaps he could go look for it. Now, it was raining, but she thought she could get him to go find it. We received a call back from Ernie about six o'clock that evening that he had it, and Ernie packed it up and shipped it back to us, and we got all of our pictures and our balloon stuff back. It's a pretty typical recovery story showing how we get balloon capsules back when they land somewhere where you don't know anybody. Thank you to Ernie in New Liberty, Iowa.

A review of the photos from that launch proved that Team Omega had set the record for the second-highest altitude for a RoboDawgs DawgTag. The DawgTags had been given out by the well-traveled robotics team for several years at that point and had been seen in more than a dozen countries. Based on the position and curvature of the Earth in the photos, the RoboDawgs put this DawgTag up to an altitude of approximately 100,000 feet.

In July, the RoboDawgs launched their next balloon in their Race to Space efforts, which carried special film in a light-proof container to study gamma-ray bursts. In August, the team launched another high-altitude balloon in a continuation of their effort to capture gamma radiation on film. The balloon spent nearly four hours aloft, and it was recovered for the team by the very helpful employees at Friedland Industries in Lansing, Michigan.

In August 2013, the RoboDawgs students were back at it with crowdfunding, this time to acquire a whole new parts-making technology. The students put together the new campaign to purchase a MakerBot® Replicator® 2X 3D printer. That technology fabricated plastic parts using additive manufacturing, building up a piece a layer at a time until it was complete. The fundraising target of $3,500 was quickly met, and the printer arrived in September. Students immediately put it to work making small, simple objects, with the team printing miniature traffic cones and a mount for a GoPro Hero camera. It didn't take long for the students to begin to learn the intricacies of 3D printing. The RoboDawgs were making parts for robots using 3D printing before the school was doing anything with them.

During the summer of 2013, the RoboDawgs used their new CNC machine to fabricate parts for a NASA rocket scheduled to launch that fall. That summer and fall, RoboDawgs completed a sixty-day effort to assist a Johns Hopkins University and University of Maryland research team that was preparing multiple scientific experiments for launch aboard a RockSatX mission. As it happened, the research leader for that team was a RoboDawg graduate. The researchers needed custom enclosures and components for their payload, and they asked the RoboDawgs to help out.

In September 2013, the RoboDawgs' third attempt at the launch and recovery of an ultra-high-altitude balloon was successful. The team recovered that most recent launch and its payload of sensors from a cornfield in northwest Ohio. A first run through the data showed that the balloon did not break the team's current 110,000-foot altitude record, but it did spend a significant period of time at an altitude where temperatures were colder than -100°F. New batteries being tested kept all the balloons sensors, trackers, and camera working throughout the long flight, and all the way back to Grandville. Also in September 2013, another weather-balloon launch yielded hundreds of photos and two hours of video from the Grandville High School Homecoming game.

Continuing their ongoing efforts to aid other programs, the RoboDawgs announced a mentoring program in the fall of 2013 designed to support Michigan high schools applying for a state grant to support a new or existing *FIRST* Robotics team. The 2013 State School Aid Act, section 99h, appropriated $3,000,000 for the 2013–2014 school year for competitive grants to districts that provided pupils in grades 7–12 with expanded opportunities to improve mathematics, science, and technology skills by participating in events hosted by *FIRST* Robotics. The Grandville RoboDawgs offered to assist new and existing teams with the preparation of grant applications, as well as the development of educational strategies, team organization, mentor development, fundraising, and robot design and construction.

That November of 2013, Mike went to the "well" of the Donors Choose program to help kickstart a new project, a second 3D printer for the RoboDawgs. From November 21 through November 28, when someone donated to fund the new printer, Donors Choose matched the donation dollar for dollar. Before the seven-day fundraising challenge was up, RoboDawgs supporters had fully funded the team's second 3D printer.

Mike: The design, testing, and redesign of parts was a great exercise in materials science for the students. They found that, by designing and printing their own custom 3D parts, they could reduce the weight of a standard FRC robot (120 pound) by more than eight pounds, without sacrificing strength or performance. We've been amazed what happens when you take a talented and motivated group of kids, train them, give them a tool, set some boundaries – and then get out of their way.

The year ended with a bang, with a final successful balloon flight. That one, launched December 28 and recovered on December 30, hit an estimated height of 130,000 feet, and traveled just under 450 miles "as the crow flies." It was recovered by friends of the team from New York state.

The RoboDawgs had a roaring start to their 2014. The January edition of the *FIRST* newsletter featured a story entitled "FRC RoboDawgs Help Teams in Michigan Form and Thrive," highlighting the program's longstanding efforts to assist other schools and communities in setting up their own academic robotics programs, and to assist their teams with parts and knowhow.

All three FRC Competition teams started the FRC season at the Toronto East Regional FRC event in Oshawa, Ontario. The RoboDawgs had a good first event for that year, and once again they brought home a trophy from the event, making it six of the last seven years that the RoboDawgs had won awards at FRC events. RoboDawgs FRC Competition Team 288 won the Gracious Professionalism Award, recognizing a team for working with and supporting other teams at the event. The RoboDawgs, by that time, had become well-known for their friendly and helpful nature, as the Toronto award marked the third time the team had won the Gracious Professionalism award in the prior six years.

Our teams played their second event of the year back in Howell, Michigan. They used their time at that event to complete some robot upgrades and to improve their game-play in preparation for their next event in Midland. Our teams all went on to do well in Midland, finishing 8th, 10th, and 16th out of 40 teams. Team 288 played all the way to the Championship, winning the event and bringing home a blue banner.

To round out the FRC season, the RoboDawgs headed back to Calgary. The program took nearly 50 varsity team members to compete in one of the best events in Canada, raising more than $58,000 to fund the trip.

Mike: Our teams learned a lot about what they needed to do to win over a few days. We had a team where nearly a third of the students were new that year, and there was a lot of robot knowledge these kids were still learning. We had a phenomenally talented senior class, but they were once again learning that it takes a team to win. We lost a few rounds over those few days when RoboDawg teams took to the field without completing their checks and maintenance between rounds. Loose power connections cost us at least three matches. An open pneumatics valve cost us a match. The only path to winning on a student–run FRC team is when the captains fully engage at least eight students and the whole group works together to keep their machine running and winning.

Meanwhile, MakerBot, the producer of the 3D printers used by the RoboDawgs, contacted the team to learn about their experiences, and then decided to feature the team on its blog. The folks at Makerbot pulled out four pieces of "3D Printing Wisdom" from the experiences the RoboDawgs shared.

In April, the program held a signing day for the RoboDawgs. Grandville High School stopped for a moment to celebrate the graduating RoboDawgs who were going on to play at the college level.

> **Mike:** I noticed that our star athletes at the high school received a great deal of attention on our video announcements when they signed on to go to a particular college or university. A signing ceremony usually accompanied that student's agreement to go and play for that school in exchange for scholarships and other benefits. It was a celebration of what the student athlete had accomplished both in high school and what they will accomplish in the future. I reasoned that our robotics students deserved similar attention, so I suggested a signing day for RoboDawgs. We know that many of our students will go on to become professional scientists or engineers in the future. Their accomplishments should also be duly and formally celebrated!

These students had proven themselves to be very good at programming competitive robots, designing mechanical arms, building racing drones, bringing concepts to life using 3D printing, and applying physics to real-world problems.

The signing day recognized 19 Grandville seniors who were going on to college to design satellites, build solar-powered planes and cars, develop power systems for rural African communities, and compete in the most advanced robotics competitions in the world. The graduating RoboDawgs that year carried an average GPA of over 3.8. Every graduating senior in the program in 2014 went on to college, and that graduating group was offered scholarships totaling more than $786,000, for an average of $41,000 in scholarship offers received by the graduating RoboDawgs – a new team record. Sixteen of the graduates went on to major in STEM areas.

Our coaches also started our annual VEX Summer Camp at Camp Newaygo in the summer of 2014. They had been looking for an overnight engineering summer camp that would allow both boys and girls to attend for a couple years. They decided in the fall of 2013 that, if we wanted an engineering camp that girls could attend, we would have to start our own. Searching for the ideal camp, Camp Newaygo popped up on the radar. It is a well-established camp with a full summer staff, with a lake and trails. They had archery and tye-dying, and ropes-challenge courses. The only issue – Camp Newaygo had been a girls-only camp for almost 90 years. We were thrilled that they welcomed us with open arms – as long as we came during their shoulder season when they did not have regular summer sessions running at the camp. Doug and Mike ran full two camps that summer, one the week of June 22 and one the week of August 17. That year, a RoboDawg tradition was started that has stood through every year since. The young women – and young men – on the RoboDawgs team attend camp together to run and swim, and program and compete with robots.

In September, thanks to the teams' summer fundraising, the Robodawgs were flying a new quadcopter built by team members during August. Carrying the name *RoboDawg 1*, this aircraft provided the first opportunity for students to learn about autonomous flight. They used the same autopilot software they had used in the autonomous boat race for the previous three years, which provided valuable experience. Early test flights helped students understand *RoboDawg 1*'s speed and flight range, and how it handled in strong winds.

Our RoboDawgs started their second full VEX season in the fall of 2014.

The November 2014 issue of *National Science Teachers Association (NTSA) Reports* recognized the accomplishments of the program, and several RoboDawgs alumni graced the front page. The NTSA devoted the entire front page, as well as an inside page, to their article "Teaming Science and Robotics."

On December 6, 2014, the RoboDawgs hosted their first annual Holiday VEX tournament. Forty-four teams came from all over Michigan to play at the Grandville Robotics and Engineering Center, making this the largest 2014 VEX event in Michigan. The RoboDawgs put up the holiday lights and put on music from the season as teams played in more than 60 seeding rounds throughout the morning and early afternoon. This was the first event to be livestreamed from the Robotics and Engineering Center.

RISE OF THE ROBODAWGS: 2015–2022

As we started 2015, the RoboDawgs had come through several key inflection points. We were coming off the 2013–2014 year, which was one of our best ever. Our largest class of graduating seniors had moved on to college in the summer of 2014, taking with them a great deal of talent and knowledge, so we began a period of rebuilding. We had a good VEX season the prior fall and qualified seven teams for the VEX State Championship in February, 2015. We were State Championship finalists, which was the best finish in our short history.

The 2015 FRC game, "Recycle Rush," was among our least favorite over the years. Teams were confined to their alliance's half of the field, and the game consisted of stacking tote and trash cans. We played four events that year, followed the by *FIRST* Championship in St. Louis.

> **Mike:** This was an unremarkable FRC year, probably because of the game. But we did establish a new RoboDawgs policy as a result of the team's poor attendance at the Windsor event.

> **Doug:** Wow – that event began on the first day of

Spring Break that year. Kids signed up to attend this event and we booked hotel rooms and made meal reservations for all the members of our three teams, as well as chaperones and coaches. Then, the week of the event, students began to inform us that they would not be coming to Windsor with the team.

Mike: Almost a third of the team ended up backing out of this trip – some on the day we left for Windsor. We incurred several thousand dollars in costs for students who changed their minds and did not end up going to this event. We have always been opposed to "pay-to-play" policies, where only students whose parents could write a large check could participate, but we could not incur these types of costs again. So – our "pay-not-to-play" policy came into existence.

Doug: Ever since 2015, the permission slips for students attending events with significant committed costs includes the language: "We will commit to transportation, hotel rooms, and other costs which cannot be recovered once we commit to this trip. Once this permission slip is completed, the student is committed to attend this event if invited. Parents of students who opt not to attend will be expected to reimburse the team for per-person trip."

Mike: This policy totally changed the game. There have been very few students who have committed to a robotics competition trip since 2015 and then backed out.

In April 2015, the RoboDawgs completed their first launch in connection with the 2015 Global Space Balloon Challenge. This was a "typical" RoboDawg high-altitude balloon launch, coordinated with the schedule for the Space Balloon Challenge.

In September, the RoboDawgs had a busy night at the Homecoming football game. One group took the team's mobile football canon, while a second group of RoboDawgs flew one of the team's quadcopters. As usual, the football shooter was a big hit. With a range of nearly 200 yards, the football canon mounted on a RoboDawg robot delivered foam footballs to all corners of the bleachers.

The team's quadcopters continued to accumulate successful flight hours in and around Grandville High School events during 2015. The RoboDawgs followed the Grandville High School Marching Band, and the team took still photos and video that were compiled in a promotional video for the band.

The RoboDawgs VEX program continued to grow and mature in the fall of 2015. We split our VEX League into two timeframes, hosting an early fall and a late fall VEX League. We ran a November VEX tournament and our annual Holiday VEX event in December. Our teams continued to improve, and we qualified nine teams for the 2016 State Championship.

The 2016 FRC season was shorter for the RoboDawgs – we only played in three events. We were still rebuilding talent lost in the big graduating class of 2014, and our teams were not ready for more. We played our first event in St. Joseph and then moved on to our home event at Grand Valley State University. The teams showed great progress at this West Michigan District event, with Team 216 – More

RoboDawgs – playing all the way to the semi-finals. The teams later sent their robots off to Calgary, where they played in the Western Canada Regional FRC tournament, held in the Olympic Oval.

That April, the RoboDawgs continued the trend for the program's alumni to build and program fun things after they graduate and move on to college. Two graduates became members of the Purdue Orbital team, where they took part in a test launch in southwest Michigan. It was the first launch for the Purdue Orbital team as they pursued a goal of putting 5 kg in space by 2018. The ground launch of the 9-foot test rocket was a success, launching on cue and hitting a top speed of more than 1,100 mph on its way to a maximum altitude of more than a mile. All systems functioned as planned, and the rocket popped its parachutes on the way down to a soft landing.

In June 2016, the RoboDawgs continued to work on technology to achieve sustained flight with high-altitude balloons. The team's rising sophomores and juniors put up a launch to test a new method for releasing the capsule when the balloon crossed a specific geofence. The test was not successful, but the balloon did become the team's first to drop its capsule in another country – Canada! As always, photos of the flight were captured. By this time, every flight captured thousands of new images, and the RoboDawgs flight image library numbered more than 250,000 near space images.

By the end of 2016, the VEX Robotics program in West Michigan had continued to grow dramatically. Thanks to the efforts of parents and organizers, more than a dozen new competitive robotics programs had sprung up in school districts all over the state. Over the previous three years, major VEX Robotics programs had started in schools all around the Grandville area, including the public-school systems in Hudsonville, Jenison, Grand Rapids, Kenowa Hills, Caledonia, and Portage, along with Grand Rapids Christian Schools. VEX Robotics, by that time, was the largest competitive robotics program in the world, with more than 590 teams in Michigan alone.

This rapid growth had put pressure on event organizers all over Michigan to expand the capacity of their VEX tournaments. Only two years previously, it was common to hold 24-team tournaments in West Michigan. That year, events had huge waitlists and it had become common to run events hosting twice that many teams.

In the previous three years, there had been a well-attended Halloween VEX tournament in West Michigan. In the fall of 2016, Grandville signed up to host the next annual Halloween tournament and the waitlist quickly grew. The Robodawgs first cut the registration off at 36 teams, then increased it to 48 teams, and finally let another 7 teams in from the waitlist to bring the event up to 55 teams. But that quickly led to the question of where the program would hold the event.

Grandville Public Schools had been tremendously supportive of the RoboDawgs program, particularly under superintendents Ron Caniff and Roger Bearup. The program had the biggest and best robotics center in the state of Michigan, regularly hosting 30-40 teams for weekly robotics league play. The Robotics Center, however, could not accommodate 55 teams. So the coaches started to look around the district for space. Grandville Public Schools is one of the top-rated districts in the state, and you can see one of the reasons why when you start to look for competition space in our buildings. The high school had four major events scheduled on the date of the Halloween tournament, as well as a dozen practice times for sports, the fall play, and activities with other student groups. The middle school was completely booked, as were the gyms and multipurpose rooms at elementary schools across the district. This is one busy district, and the buildings were very highly utilized at the time. Where were they going to hold this huge Halloween tournament?

> **Doug:** The Halloween VEX tournament in 2016 is one of the iconic RoboDawg stories. We have always had unreasonable belief, and this event called to us. Mike, you uttered one of those famous quotes from the team's history as we discovered that there was nowhere – absolutely nowhere – in the district that we could hold this event.

> **Mike:** Why don't we do it in a tent? It just came out of my mouth.

As usual, the answer came from Mike. A founder of the Grandville robotics program in 1998, and a high school physics teacher who can think so far outside the box that people often wonder if there is a box, he asked, "Why don't we do it in a tent?"

And so they did. On Saturday, October 29, the RoboDawgs hosted the tournament inside a giant circus tent erected outside the Grandville Robotics and Engineering Center. Bleachers were erected and level floors were built up to support competition and practice fields. Lights were hung, field electronics were installed, and power and wireless internet were extended into the tent, using nearly a mile of power and ethernet cable. Tent heaters were brought in, and more than 500 feet of runner was put down to keep teams from walking on the muddy ground. They even brought in popcorn and slushy machines!

> **Mike:** Every now and then, we see the team pull off amazing things. With just a bit of direction from the coaches, the students built the flooring, figured out the lighting, and assembled this very unique tournament. When you have a large group of smart, well-motivated students, you are wise to give them some direction and get out of their way. I've always been amazed at what the team can accomplish when they put their minds to it.

It was at this event that the Grandville Superintendent Roger Bearup suggested that, perhaps, the district should help us find some dedicated competition space. This seems to have been the turning point leading to our next big change in the program. This story will continue in Chapter 7.

Our VEX program that year was about more than just a Halloween event. The state needed more events that fall, so in addition to the Halloween tournament, we hosted three Fall Leagues and our annual Holiday VEX tournament. More than 100 teams attended the Holiday tournament, once again making it the largest event in Michigan that year. We had a great fall, qualifying twelve teams for the 2016 VEX State Championship.

In February 2017, Mike Evele once again tapped into Donors Choose, completing the funding needed for three new 3D printers within four hours. That brought the RoboDawgs family of 3D printers to eight machines from five manufacturers. The teams could print in nylon, fiberglass, PLA, HIP, PET, ABS, and carbon fiber. The fleet of 3D printers was running close to 24 hours a day to churn out parts for the *FIRST* Robotics Competition robots. A large group of RoboDawgs worked with the machines, led by a small group of dedicated students who worked with the 3D printers and the CNC machine every week throughout the year.

Also in February, the RoboDawgs competed in the State VEX Robotics Championship. Twelve high school and six middle school teams qualified and played. That day turned out to be a Dawgs day at Michigan State University. RoboDawgs were on the winning alliance and the finalist alliance. This was the first time the RoboDawgs had ever won the State Championship AND taken second place! They also won the State Skills Challenge. Six of the twelve State Championship teams qualified to play at the VEX World Championship in April. Those six teams claimed a state and national record, as no other public high school in America had ever before qualified six teams for the World Championship.

We had a great FRC season in 2017 as we continued to rebuild talent. We started the season playing in Victoria Park, Ontario. Our teams next played in Lansing, where Team 244 played all the way to the finals, with their alliance finishing in second place. We played at our home event in East Kentwood, and then headed back to Calgary. The RoboDawgs were well-known at this event, hosted in the Olympic Oval. This was the last year the event was held in the Olympic Oval, and our teams played to make it count. Team 244 really rose to the occasion, playing all the way to the finals. Again at this event, 244's alliance lost in the finals, leaving them in second place. Teams that beat them in the finals were already qualified for the FRC Championship in St. Louis, so a wildcard invitation was extended to team 244. We accepted and went on to play well at the Championship. Team 244 finished 17th out of 73 teams in their division.

That April, Grandville High School sent off more than two dozen RoboDawgs and mentors to the VEX World Championship in Louisville, Kentucky. On their way to this accomplishment, RoboDawg teams were champions or finalists in eleven tournaments and leagues, and they won both the West Michigan Regional Championship and the Michigan VEX Robotics State Championship.

Mike and Doug ran the annual VEX Summer Camp at Camp Newaygo that year. It became clear that VEX Camp was not just for Grandville and area students anymore. The camp began attracting students from as far north as Traverse City and as far south as Kentucky.

Our VEX program continued to build capability, and we continued to host more, and larger, events. Grandville hosted three VEX Leagues, two Halloween tournaments, and our annual Holiday VEX tournament in December – which drew a record 116 teams. During the fall, we qualified a record 12 RoboDawg teams for the 2018 VEX State Championship.

Sadly, October 28, 2017, brought a terrible loss to the Grandville community, when its former high school principal, Chris VanderSlice, died of cancer. His passing was an especially painful loss for the robotics community.

Doug: Chris VanderSlice passed away after a nearly four-year battle with leukemia. I knew Chris for nineteen years, and I have hundreds of personal experiences with him in all kinds of situations.

Chris was always seeking the best for everyone around him. He had energy to match his height, and I saw him take on everything – he never faded from the pursuit of what was right. He had a passion for young people, and I watched him tirelessly advocate for students. Chris was an inspiration to so many of us. His strength of character and commitment to our young people inspired me. His encouragement and support inspired thousands of students. Most people don't know this, but Chris was a huge proponent of the Grandville robotics program. In 2009, a group of our sixth-graders signed on to play Botball – a robotics competition primarily for high school students. Chris was an assistant principal at the middle school, and he thought this was a great challenge for these young people. Our young students went on to place in the top three teams at a regional event in St. Louis, earning them an opportunity to play at the National Championship in Washington D.C. This event was over the 4th of July, when many school employees are getting some time away, but Chris was right there with us. I learned a lot from the way Chris lived his life over the years, but his approach to facing cancer had an even bigger impact on me (and thousands of students). "Grit" became a standard part of everyone's view of life, and the grit Chris displayed in fighting cancer was an example for all of us. Losing Chris leaves a huge pair of shoes to fill. The world has too few legends, but he certainly was a legendary leader to those around him.

We unexpectedly hosted our first Middle School and High School State VEX Championships at Grandville High School on February 25, 2018. While we had been running the largest VEX events in the region for several years, Michigan State University had always hosted the State Championships. That year, heavy rains and melting snow brought the Red Cedar river up over its banks, flooding the area around MSU's Jenison Fieldhouse. Three days prior to the Championships, we were asked to take the event on and host it in Grandville. Our volunteers really showed what we are capable of, as plans came together quickly to host both the High School and Middle School Championships in Grandville. The three days leading up to the event were a whirl of activity, but our RoboDawgs played well and we won the High School State Championship for a second year in a row, adding another Champions banner to our wall. A RoboDawg team also won the State of Michigan Excellence Award – the highest award given by VEX – for the first time.

Our FRC teams had really improved over the prior two years, and we decided to accept an invitation to compete at the Hawaii Regional FRC tournament. This was our first time playing outside the continental U.S. and the trip would take our students out of school for ten days. We played only two other FRC events that year, in St. Joseph and Kentwood, Michigan.

Preparation for the Hawaii event began in the prior fall. Fundraising was a key activity, and we raised money from every source we could find. Two large donors helped a lot, and a local family made a special contribution so our team could attend a traditional Hawaiian Luau.

We had a clear focus on our students' academic performance during the 2017–2018 school year. In the fall, we had agreed with our team members that they would need to have an unweighted 3.5 GPA in their core classes to travel with the team to Hawaii. Our study hall was popular all year – even at our poolside sessions in Hawaii. Students supported each other, and tutors helped some students who needed a little extra assistance. We were very proud of the team – every student on the team met the higher minimum-grade requirement and traveled with us to Hawaii.

We had a great time there – and not just because our team 244 was on the winning alliance and brought home another blue banner for our wall. We were particularly pleased to be picked to play in the finals with The Hawaiian Kids, FRC Team 359. We have played at many events with this outstanding team, and won an event with them again in 2024.

Students did very will being away from home for that long period and we were able to spend some time enjoying the island of O'ahu. When we travel, we aim to compete well, to do some things that are educational, and to do some things that are fun.

After Hawaii, we had our annual awards night and then eased into summer. During the summer of 2018, Mike and Doug ran the VEX Summer Camp. They also ran a summer VEX program for our teams. This was our first year playing VEX during the summer, and we built and programmed robots to play at our first county fair event in Monroe, Michigan.

August of 2018 saw the RoboDawgs continuing their winning ways at the Monroe County Fair event, the first Michigan VEX Robotics tournament of the 2018–2019 season. Our teams played well and enjoyed the rides on the midway. The teams had a great day, with two of them winning the event and bringing home another set of champion trophies. The end of our stay at the fair was anti-climatic. We watched the slow-motion action in a combine demolition derby. Watching giant farm vehicles try to destroy each other was not as exciting as we had hoped.

The following month, the RoboDawgs continued with their pet photography projects. While the Grandville football team notched its third win of the season, the RoboDawgs again had their drones in the air, taking pictures and video of the team and the Marching Band. As always, safe drone operation was the priority.

> **Mike:** It was a challenging night to fly, with some moderately gusty winds, and our team had to modify its normal flight protocols to make sure we flew safely. The team completed its pre-game test flights at 4pm and identified a new launch site outside the football stadium and downwind of the crowds. All our flightpaths that night took into account the direction and strength of the wind, with our take-off, landing, and emergency return-to-home landing paths all avoiding areas where people might be. We had to make sure that, if the wind caused a flight failure, we would not be in a position to be over people at any point. The preparations paid off, and we had a great night of flights, booking almost two hours of flight time.

Fall 2018 started our biggest VEX season ever. We had more kids and more teams than in any prior year – and we hosted new events. This was the year we joined with Hudsonville and Jenison to start the new West Michigan Mega League.

This 20-night league was developed to support the growing number of West Michigan VEX teams. More than 90 West Michigan teams had the option to compete on any Tuesday, Wednesday, or Thursday night from October 4 to November 20. Three host sites (Hudsonville, Grandville, and Jenison) and three competition nights each week meant that teams could fit their competition nights around other commitments and activities. It allowed us to accommodate 92 teams that year – and it could scale to support more than 150 teams in future years.

We still hosted our Halloween and Holiday VEX events, and the Holiday VEX event was once again the largest event held in Michigan that year. Seeing the need for a late event, we added our New Year's VEX tournament on the first weekend in January.

Our program continued to pivot from VEX to FRC in January. While we were building our FRC robots, we worked hard to keep our VEX teams sharp, playing internal scrimmages each week.

We had an excellent outing at the VEX High School State Championship in late February. The RoboDawgs qualified more teams for the championship than we ever had – or that we have since. Fifteen RoboDawg teams qualified to play at this event and we had another excellent outing. Our teams played all the way into the finals, losing there to finish second in the state. A RoboDawg team won the Excellence Award for the second straight year. We also posted the highest score at the Championship and brought home the Skills Champion banner.

Our FRC teams were playing the "Destination Deep Space" game, throwing rubber cargo balls into rocket ships and putting hatch covers in place. This was the second year that Disney imagineers had helped *FIRST* with game design and branding – and it showed. While it was not one of our favorite games, our teams did well. We started our competition season at the St. Joseph District tournament. Team 288 played all the way to the finals, and their alliance won the event. Another blue banner came home for our wall.

We moved on the the Georgian College event in Barrie, Ontario. All our teams played well. All of them finished in the top 12 teams, and all three were alliance captains! We were knocked out of the playoff in the quarter-finals, but we had a great time in Barrie!

Our final event of 2019 was back home at Kentwood. This is always a hard event, with the best teams in the state playing here. Professional engineers loved this event because the level of play here was often higher than at the State Championship. We played well, and finished our season here.

We held our annual award night in May and took our year-end trip to Chicago to eat deep-dish pizza, play whirlyball, and ride the coasters at Great America.

It was a busy summer for the RoboDawgs. We had Summer VEX Camp at Camp Newaygo in June, and then jumped right into a busy Summer VEX schedule. We were excited about county-fair events – they gave us a chance to play in front of the public and we got to figure the VEX game out early in the season. We built and programmed every week that summer, and played at two county-fair events.

Our 2019–2020 VEX competition season started at the Monroe County Fair. RoboDawgs teams once again won the event, and we were finalists. It was a great start to what would become one of our best VEX years ever. The season continued to show signs of promise when we played at the

Hudsonville Community Fair event two weeks later. RoboDawgs teams won this event, giving us a perfect summer-fair record. At this point, RoboDawgs teams had won every fair event we had ever played at.

We had what had become a typical fall VEX season. We worked with Hudsonville, Jenison – and now Caledonia – to host the West Michigan Mega League. More than 100 teams played more than 700 matches over 20 League nights. Again this year, RoboDawgs teams won the Mega League championship. We hosted our Halloween, Holiday, and New Year's VEX events.

November 9, 2019 was a day of firsts for our 22-year-old robotics program. On that day, RoboDawgs Team 244A won a VEX Signature event at the Indianapolis Motor Speedway. Signature events were new, and they brought together the best VEX teams across a region. This was our first-ever Signature event, and we won a surprise upset victory, beating the #1 ranked alliance captained by the team with the top Skills Challenge score in the world. RoboDawgs teams had played on multiple events on the same day in different cities – but this was the first time we had won events in two cities on the same day. While our Team 244A was winning in Indianapolis, our eams 288C and 248A won the West Michigan Fall tournament our program was hosting at Grandville High School. To really put the icing on the day, two RoboDawgs teams put up Skills Challenge scores placing them in the top 30 teams in the World Rankings on the same day. Oh, and RoboDawgs Team 248A won the Excellence Award – VEX's highest award – at the West Michigan Fall tournament. This was a day for the record books.

In October, Gov. Gretchen Whitmer approved all 16 state budget bills passed by the Michigan Legislature. That included nearly $5 million in state grant money to support competitive robotics teams (like the RoboDawgs) in public schools. This budget continued the 99(h) robotics grant funding that provides over $100k in funding for our Grand-ville robotics programs each year.

Doug: Later that fall, in November, our work to pass a bond millage which included funding for a new robotics competition center came to a head. On the first Tuesday in November, local voters approved a ballot initiative providing funding for a new middle school, which was much-needed due to population growth in the city. The plans for that new school included a purpose-built facility for robotics. That addition provided for much-need-ed competition space, an expansion of the digital fabrication lab, an elementary STEM lab, and a technology collaboration center where teams of all ages could work together to solve design and build challenges. The passing of this millage set things in motion for the sixth key inflection point for our program: the 2023 opening of the Grand-ville Robotics Competition Center.

Doug: Our robotics parents worked for months to build support for the 2019 bond millage. We all knew this was a really important vote for our pro-gram. We needed to pass a $94-million bond pro-posal. We spent election day working the phones and getting everyone we knew out to vote. I was making calls right up until the polls closed. The vote ended up being very close – 3,773 voting YES and 3,657 voting NO. After all the work we put in, this proposal passed by just 116 votes. We had talked about that election as being a once-in-a-lifetime opportunity, and it might just have been. The COVID pandemic arrived less than six months after this important vote, and had we not passed this bond proposal (on the first try), who knows when we might next have been able to do so.

In December 2019, the RoboDawgs hosted the 1st annual Midwest Elite VEX Championship at Grandville Middle School. The event brought together the top VEX Robotics teams from Michigan, Indiana, Ohio, and Illinois to play for bragging rights as the Midwest Elite VEX Champion. It also featured a special trophy.

Doug: As we were planning for this first annual event, our organizers were contemplating a trophy worthy of this level of competition. Something old and interesting that would be valued over many years as the property of that year's winner of this regional invitational event. The Old Brass Spittoon and the Old Oaken Bucket came to mind. VEX events are won by alliances of two teams, so we needed two of whatever we came up with. Team coaches and supporters searched the country, eventually coming across a pair of antique brass boots at Jon Beasley Antiques, in Cookeville, Tennessee. More than 50 years old, these solid brass boots polished up nicely! The boots found their way onto beautiful walnut bases, and will now live on as traveling trophies for the Midwest VEX Elite event.

In January 2020, the RoboDawgs were headed into a year unlike any other. We started our FRC season the first Saturday in January, while keeping our VEX teams active. They made their annual trip to compete at the Kalahari Resort in Sundusky, Ohio in January, 2020. Nine of our teams made this trip, and we played all the way into the finals. We were excited to finish this event in second place. All our teams played well, which made us fell good about our prospects at the State of Michigan Championship in February.

In mid-February, during the peak of FRC build season, we traveled with all our RoboDawgs teams to play a VEX tournament in Crown Point, Indiana. This event was intended to warm them back up for the State Championship. While we did not win the event, it did fire our teams up and launched us into a period of intense preparation for the upcoming State Championship.

On February 23, we played at the State of Michigan High School VEX Championship at Michigan State University. Eighteen RoboDawgs teams qualified for the Championship that year, and we dominated on and off the playing field. The State finals were RoboDawg vs. RoboDawg. Our teams were Champions, finalists, and semi-finalists at the event. A RoboDawgs team had the top skills score and brought home the Skill Champion banner. We won the Amaze and Build Awards – and the Excellence Award for the second straight year. No program in America had ever dominated a State Championship like this.

As we head into March, 2022, COVID-19 comes into the scene. Like the rest of the world, the RoboDawgs had new challenges and uncertainties to navigate.

We were scheduled to travel to Seattle on March 3, 2020, and then on to Victoria, British Columbia for the Canadian

Pacific Regional FRC tournament from March 4–7. This was out first trip to play at the event, held in Victoria, British Columbia, and we were preparing to travel as the United States was starting to talk about COVID-19. On February 28th, Seattle reported the nation's first coronavirus-related fatality, and Roger Bearup had sent a district-wide email explaining that Kent ISD and our school districts had been in touch with the Kent County Health Department regarding coronavirus concerns and precautions. No specific plans or guidance were available yet, but a discussion had begun. We discussed our upcoming trip to Victoria with Roger and provided our plans for various scenarios that might play out. He gave us permission to continue with our plans to compete in Victoria the following week.

We flew into Seattle with Delta Airlines on Tuesday, March 3, passing through Detroit and Minneapolis airports. The planes were fairly full, and the airports were busy. There were one or two school districts north of Seattle that had closed their schools for up to two weeks, and both were in a pocket where there had been a large number of people impacted by the virus in a nursing home. That nursing home had been quarantined for several days.

We spent the night in Seattle, and took the team to Victoria Island on the morning of March 4. That night, we moved into the Save-On Center for the FRC event. We had a great start to the event there, as the world around us began to focus on the developing coronavirus story.

On March 5 and 6, news reports across the country raised concerns about our group being so far from home. Articles in *The New York Times* – "Empty Jets and Deserted Airports: Coronavirus rattles an Industry" – and the *Wall Street Journal* – "Schools Shut in Seattle Area as Coronavirus

Spreads" – got everyone in Grandville talking about our teams. We had conversations where we considered leaving the competition early and flying the team home.

There were no known cases of the coronavirus in Victoria, where we were competing. There were no teams at the event from any Seattle-area school or community with known coronavirus cases – or from Japan, Korea, Iran, Italy, or China. Despite the sensational headlines in the news, domestic flights at the time continued to fly every day. The largest reduction in domestic flights reported so far had been a 10% reduction by United. We did not believe we would have difficulty flying home. There were no reported coronavirus cases in Victoria, and there were no significant cases in the area of Seattle we had visited. We concluded that, with some additional precautions, we could keep the team safe and allow them to complete the competition. We extended our stay in Victoria, and cancelled plans to spend a day sightseeing in Seattle on our way home. We had meals brought into the hotel and ate other meals in areas of restaurants that had been sectioned off from us, reducing contact with people not with our team. When it was time to return home, we traveled from Victoria to a hotel at the Seattle airport, and then went straight home from there. We bought gallons of hand sanitizer and our team washed their hands at every opportunity.

In the end, we returned home on March 10 without anyone contracting COVID-19. The trip had been a great success, and it was the last fun these kids would have for three months. It would end up being their last FRC competition for two years.

Doug: The next inflection point for our program

really comes when Michigan schools closed down on March 12 due to COVID-19.

Mike: Yes. COVID-19 changed everything, but instead of shutting down, our program changed and grew as we innovated around COVID-19.

The pandemic hit the world like a ton of bricks. Schools closed, and many extracurricular activities shut down as well.

The RoboDawgs didn't. The program remained active through the stay-at-home period in Michigan and kept students engaged using virtual meetings, challenges, Zoom sessions, and remote 3D printing. Much of the program's funding was in jeopardy due to the impact of the coronavirus pandemic, so the teams came up with their own solution. The RoboDawgs began collecting returnable cans and bottles to fund their summer programs, working toward a goal of 100,000 cans and bottles in May. (In Michigan, most beverage bottles and cans come with a ten-cent deposit, which the purchaser can get back by returning the empty container.)

> **Mike:** I predicted the incredible number of returnable cans we would get. During a call that April, I told Doug, "If we do this, you realize we're going to end up buried in cans." I said, "There's that old quote from the movie *Tora, Tora, Tora,* where the Japanese general says, 'We have awoken a sleeping giant and filled him with a terrible resolve.'" That's what we did. We ended up waist-deep in cans. Our program was such a success that the *Wall Street Journal* wrote an article about us.

Students set up a huge collection bin at the Grandville Robotics Center and requested that area residents donate their empty returnables to support the Grandville robotics teams. When retail stores were forced to stop accepting cans and bottles during the pandemic, the RoboDawgs proceeded to bag and store more than 500,000 returnables to help keep their programs running during the summer and fall.

Our teams collected more than a million returnables in 2020, and we've continued that fundraising activity ever since.

As the pandemic went on and shutdowns were eased, the RoboDawgs made every effort to begin in-person activities as early as possible. They got back to their operations in June 2020 with the start of summer VEX camps. The RoboDawgs purchased seven 20'x40' tents and began summer activities outdoors under them. The camps were fully booked, with parents excited to get their kids back to activities. Grandville was one of the first programs in the country to hold in-person summer camps, and it was a busy summer, with kids from all school levels building robots and competing outdoors.

We successfully ran a safe camp in August 2020 that generated no COVID-19 transmissions and allowed these kids to get together, build robots, and have fun swimming, kayaking, and doing ziplines. Our success gave us hope for the fall season. We held our first VEX event that involved multiple teams from multiple states on August 22, outdoors at our robotics center. It was held in tents, including all the teams' pits.

Doug: We did not wear masks at camp, but we kept kids in these groups of ten. Those were the groups they stayed with in a cabin, built robots with, and ate with. We also tried to do as much as we could outdoors. All our building and program sessions were done in tents, and our competition field was outdoors under a tent. We ate outdoors under tents. The students slept in open-air cabins with screen sides.

Many school districts had banned all extracurricular activities that year, and the RoboDawgs once again led the way with their rules and procedures, including social distancing and masking as required. The program set up protocols for indoor operations in buildings with enhanced airflow, and conducted build sessions and competitions by using pods and limiting contact between groups, and by limiting participation to team members. By October, 2020, our programs were back in full operation.

> **Doug:** Robotics program leaders worked with the Department of Health and Human Services and convinced State of Michigan officials not to close the Grandville Robotics program, as it was one of the safest places a student could be. This program served hundreds of students every day in the fall of 2020, and the program successfully operated from its reopening on June 6 with ZERO coronavirus transmissions.

The Grandville Robotics program proved that they could beat COVID-19. As of October, our programs had operated for 24 consecutive weeks without even a single case where one program participant passed COVID-19 to another. This was not a small accomplishment. We operated day camps and overnight camps with students from Michigan and surrounding states. We ran more than 70 elementary, middle school, and high school teams in Grandville Public Schools. We ran multiple high school competitions at our facility, bringing together top teams from six states. We ran elementary and middle school LEGO League, VEX IQ, and VEX EDR competitions for hundreds of students. And yet, through the determined efforts of our families and tight health protocols, we had NO COVID-19 transmissions in any of our programs during 2020.

Unfortunately, that November – on Friday the 13th, fittingly enough – Michigan's governor once again issued a stay-at-home order. The new restrictions ran to January 6, 2021.

The coaches worked actively with the county and state health authorities, building on the protocols they had developed through the year, to establish a set of operating guidelines for restarting our programs on January 6, 2021. Our program became a model for coronavirus precautions that were adopted at facilities and competitions around the country. We pioneered health screening and contact-tracing programs for youth teams. We used masks, social-distancing, small-group cohorts, and enhanced cleaning practices to reduce the risk of passing the coronavirus. Our facility was a closed environment, and only screened and approved team members and coaches could enter. We did not have spectators at any of our events, so we learned to broadcast our elementary, middle school, and high school leagues and tournaments on the internet so families and fans could watch.

The protocols approved by the state allowed the program to restart immediately after the lockdowns ended in early 2021. The VEX IQ, LEGO League, middle school VEX and drones, and high school VEX programs all operated through that spring. *FIRST* robotics struggled to find their path during COVID, and there was no FRC season in 2021. This really set *FIRST* back, and many teams we knew in the midwest and in Canada closed in 2021 – never to reopen. There were few Canadian events in 2020, and none in 2021 Almost all of the teams we had mentored in Calgary closed down and have not reopened as of the summer of 2024.

Thanks to the work of the RECF, VEX thrived during 2021. We held in-person events during the school year, and the RoboDawgs hosted both the state VEX IQ Championship in March, and the state VEX High School State Championship in April. Our teams participated in a virtual VEX World Championship from our robotics center, using the RECF's Live Remote technology.

It was commendable that everyone pulled together to have a virtual VEX world event VEX in 2021, but that event was not very satisfying. While Live Remote technology gave everyone a chance to compete during the COVID years, the Live Remote structure did not lend itself well to top-level competition between highly capable teams. Many high school VEX teams really wanted a chance to play a final in-person event that spring, so the RECF allowed key event partners around the country to run VEX End-of Season Showcase events. We held the Midwest Region showcase event in Grandville, on May 1 and 2. This turned out the be a great capstone event to close out the COVID era. Our event brought together top teams from Michigan – and some of the best teams in the country from Brecksville and Elyria (OH), Brentwood (IN), Freedom (WI) and Batavia (IL). It was a great event and it really felt good to see the top teams from the region playing together in person.

> **Mike:** We had never had a year anything like the 2020–2021 school year, but our robotics programs adapted, working closely with our administration and the Kent County Health Department. We are really proud of the virtual and in-person opportunities we created for students during that time.

In June, the program once again held a summer residential VEX camp. It was conducted under similar policies as in 2020, though in 2021, students were allowed to sleep indoors, and the cohorts of ten were no longer used. Though two students had to be turned away after testing positive for COVID before the camp began, the RoboDawgs again ran its summer program successfully, with no COVID transmissions.

We ran a very active summer VEX program, and our teams competed in both the Monroe and Hudsonville County Fair events. We ran our last VEX in the Tent event of the COVID era that August.

Going into the 2021–2022 school year, things were changing for the better. All our fall robotics programs started outdoors in our tents and moved indoors as it got cold (though the students discovered that they actually enjoyed the tents). Our fall VEX events were run indoors, and we returned to "normal" operations.

At the high school level, the RoboDawgs started very aggressively with a heavy travel schedule due to the introduction of a new RECF program, Bell Advanced Vertical Robotics (AVR). With the RoboDawgs' many years of experience with drones, this program was an excellent fit. Our teams loved the challenge of the Bell competition, and we traveled to Texas to play in a qualifying event and in the national championship. We did quite well that first year, with our team finishing third at the national championship.

Winter came and we had our first *FIRST* Robotics season since before COVID. Our kids were so excited to get to design and build *FIRST* robots. After two long seasons of VEX during the COVID period, they were a little tired of VEX at the high school level. FRC was hard, however, as we had lost a lot of skills across the high school team. Seniors in the 2022–2023 year would normally have entered the FRC competition season with experience playing in 12–14 tournaments over their first three years of high school. Their accumulated experience was really important to our teams, and we were clearly short on that experience in the winter of 2022. Our seniors that winter had played in three events in 2019, one in 2020, and none in 2021. We quickly realized the impact of the FRC experience our kids had missed out on during the COVID pandemic. We focused on building skills and experience across the team in 2022, and we planned to play at four FRC tournaments that year.

Grandville hosted the VEX IQ State Championship for both elementary and middle school levels. We played in the VEX High School State Championship and ended up as finalists, finishing second in the state.

We were excited to see the FRC competition season start, and our teams were back to play in Victoria, British Columbia. Our last FRC event prior to COVID was the Canadian Pacific Regional (in March, 2020) and our first event after COVID was the Canadian Pacific Regional (in March, 2022). The event in 2022 required that everyone had received a COVID vaccination, and we had to wear masks. But we got to have a *FIRST* season! The team once again won the Gracious Professionalism award at the Victoria FRC event. It is interesting that we were the only U.S. team to play at an FRC event in Canada during the 2021–2022 season. After the event in Canada, we played at three FRC tournaments in Michigan – in St. Joseph, Kentwood, and at Grand Valley State University.

The summer of 2022 brought another year of VEX Summer Camp, but other than that, we took the summer off. It had been a long two years, and our kids, coaches, and volunteers were ready for a break.

The fall of 2022 was a time when we continued to return to "normal." We ran all our programs indoors, without masks. That fall we had our "normal" VEX events, hosting sessions for the West Michigan MegaLeague and our Halloween, November, and Holiday tournaments. We once again participated in the Bell Drones competition, traveling to Austin, Texas for a qualifying event, and again qualified for the national championship, which we returned to Dallas for in December.

Our last activity of 2022 was our annual RoboDawgs Christmas party. The event, held at the Robotics and Engineering Center, was very well attended, with many alumni stopping by to check on the progress of the new Competition Center.

A SEISMIC SHIFT: 2023-2024

We finally moved into our new robotics facility in 2023. We share the stories of this move, not to brag, but to offer advice. Although, right now, this facility is rare – even unique – we hope this won't be the case in the future. We hope school districts across the country begin to understand the value of after-school STEM and how it enhances what happens in the classroom. We hope our facility is just one of the first, and with that in mind, we offer a record of our planning, conversations, struggles, and even battles as we built and moved into the Robotics Competition Center. The chapter also chronicles the burst of team activity that accompanied the initial year of our facility.

> **Doug:** Mike, our program has come through many inflection points. We have worked our way through the first six and here comes the big guy. Inflection point seven comes during the summer of 2023, and it is, perhaps, the biggest change in the history of our program.

> **Mike:** That summer, we moved into a new competition center attached to a brand-new middle

school, which gave us capabilities that we had never had before. We moved into a new building that has a a huge built-for-purpose robotics arena, drone-competition areas, flexible space for team pits, a digital fabrication lab, a machine shop, and lots of build space. This gave us new opportunities to attract sponsors and to innovate with robotics, not just for our district, but for teams from all over the area. This Robotics Competition Center created a place where teams could come and compete in ways they hadn't been able to before.

Doug: We took a building in 2012 and demonstrated what you could do with a little space. We created VEX leagues that supported the start of robotics programs in school districts all around Grand Rapids. We dramatically grew educational robotics in the Michigan area using that building, and as we moved into the new facility, it gave us even broader reach.

Our goals for this new space were simple: we would improve learning opportunities tied to our *FIRST* robotics teams by giving our kids greatly enhanced fabrication capabilities and return to building with all three teams in one build room. We would extend our VEX programs, creating more elementary and middle school teams that would compete here. We would enhance our already strong high school VEX teams, growing our high school V5 teams, and adding new fabrication and programming capability for our advanced VEX AI teams. We would expand the range of our programs, hosting more types of drone competitions for middle school and high school students – including drone racing. We would host new events and open up opportunities for our elementary, middle school, and high school kids to compete in robot combat.

This new Competition Center would allow us to have the the largest robotics events in the country. Not only was the facility bigger than any high school gym, we would not have to spend six to ten hours moving in and setting up for every event. We would draw teams from a broader region, giving them exposure to more robots and styles of play. Kids would learn more because they would compete more often. The build-program-compete-innovate cycle of improvement would create better robots and stronger competitors because teams would compete eight or ten times, not three or four times. This new building opened up new avenues for us and it turned out to be the most significant inflection point in the history of our program.

> **Doug:** As we entered 2023, we entered the most exciting chapter in the RoboDawgs' history. We jumped right into VEX and FRC during the winter of '23 and moved toward the opening of our new facility.

We started in January with our New Year's VEX competition on the first Saturday. Then we were off to Kalahari to compete with our high school teams. Also in January, we started our FRC season and began to build our robots with three FRC teams, still in the old Robotics and Engineering Center.

We played in the high school VEX State Championship the last weekend in February, once again returning home as State Champions. This event kicked off our travel season, and from here until the end of March, we were incredibly busy. Right on the heels of the State Championship, we left for Victoria, British Columbia on Monday, February 27. We traveled there to compete in the Canadian Pacific Regional, our first FRC event of the year. We had a great time at that event, and won that event with FRC Team 359, The Hawaiian Kids. We returned home on March 6, and on March 11, hosted the VEX IQ State Championship. The following weekend, we were off to London, Ontario for our next FRC event, and the weekend after that, we played at the Lakeview FRC District event. We wrapped up our FRC season at Kentwood the last weekend of March.

We had our most recent silent auction on March 28 that year. It was a lot of work, and we found that with our other fundraising efforts, this fundraiser might not continue every year. In April of 2023, we traveled to compete in VEX Worlds from the 25th to the 30th. This event was again in Dallas, Texas, and we did quite well, participating in the playoffs in our divisions. In May, we had our annual awards dinner, and in June, we took our customary year-end trip to play whirlyball and visit Great America. We returned from Chicago to head for the summer camp at Camp Newaygo.

> **Doug:** Mike, that brings us to July 2023, and now we're staring down the move into the new building.

> **Mike:** Yes. The new building wasn't quite ready for us, but the old building needed to be cleared out so that it could be renovated in time for elementary robotics.

> **Doug:** We were going to move the high school program into the new facility, but as part of the transition, the district was going to prep the old

Robotics and Engineering Center to be used by elementary teams. We had to move everything out of all the rooms by July 8, so they had time to clean the carpets and paint, and do the other upgrade work they wanted to do so the elementary kids could start in the fall.

Mike: Moving out of a robotics center is like moving out of your house. You have no idea how much stuff you've collected over the years until you decide to pick it up and move it across the street.

Doug: It was literally moving across the street. It was you, and I, my wife Rosemary, and fifty high school RoboDawgs during a very warm July.

Mike: We put everything on wheels, and we rolled it over!

Doug: Of course, when we got to the new building, we had nowhere to put it.

Mike: Exactly. Nothing was finished at the new building. We had some storage rooms, but we had no shelving, no cabinetry — no permanent homes for all that stuff.

Doug: It was quite a move. Think about moving between homes, and the new home has no kitchen cupboards yet and no shelves in the garage, and there's no doors on the rooms. We had to be out of one building, but the new building was a little behind and it was not ready for us.

Mike: Right. It was a matter of just piling everything up against the wall and dealing with it later.

The new Competition Center would dramatically change how the RoboDawgs prepared for competitions they were hosting.

Doug: This new building really represented a significant shift in our program. It was the first time we were going to work and run our programs in a building that was built for purpose.

Mike: Yes. In the history of robotics programs, most teams end up in somebody's classroom or in a shop space, and everyone tends to have to mold their program to fit the space that's available. Finally, in this case, we had the opportunity to do exactly the opposite. We had molded our space to fit the needs of our program.

Doug: If you think about events, the biggest hurdle for most organizations to have an event is they have to move everything. We used to hold large events in the gymnasiums at the high school or middle school.

Mike: We had to wait for the gymnasium to be free, and then we had to unload multiple trailers containing all the equipment and fields – everything that was required to hold a tournament.

Doug: In most cases, we moved into the high school on Friday afternoon and evening. We'd start after school, loading trailers at the Robotics Center. We'd load and move two or three trailers with up to 5,000 pounds of gear. We'd roll it into the high school. We'd set up all the competition fields. We'd set up all the pit tables and chairs.

We'd set up the concession stand. We'd set up everything we needed to run an event in both of the gyms and in the cafeteria, and many times, set up pits in the hallways. Then on Saturday night, when the event concluded, we took it all back down, put it back in the trailer, and spent a few hours hauling it back to the Robotics Center. It is such a different approach to events when you can walk in, turn on the lights, and play on fields that are already set up.

How do you design a for-purpose Robotics Competition Center? What should you think about? What conversations will you need to have with architects who are used to designing traditional school buildings?

Doug: Let's talk about this new building and the features of this building that make what we do possible. We started to design this building in 2016 and we spent many years talking about what we might need. As we got closer and the public approved the bonds in the fall of 2019, we began to work with the architects. The first plans were really quite entertaining. Do you remember the first set of plans, where the only entrance for robots was on the second floor?

Mike: I do remember that, and I do remember the conversation we had with the architects – that this just was not going to work. They didn't think that one small entrance on the second floor was a big deal.

Doug: We learned that it is difficult to design space

for robotics teams when you don't know what robotics teams do. In the summer of 2020, we made a video. We brought in a crew of RoboDawgs and we lined up everything we would typically take to an FRC event. Then we started the camera and wheeled everything out through the doors of our old robotics center. We then wheeled it back in and videoed the whole thing. It's still on the internet, by the way. We created a YouTube video for the architects showing them how we move into an FRC event.

Mike: With that visual, they quickly realized the need for overhead garage doors, and the fact you can't carry everything up and down the stairs.

Doug: Mike, there were a lot of conversations and we did a lot of work with the architects, but we got some things absolutely right. Let's talk about some of the features of this building that other people should think about as they build their own competition centers.

Mike: One thing we did right was the flooring. We have a polished concrete floor instead of a traditional wooden gym floor. Some administrators thought we should have a wooden floor just in case we want to play basketball on it, but robots are really hard on wood floors. The concrete floor we have can take just about anything. You can drop a robot on it, and you don't have to worry about scratching it. This is the floor you need for robotics competitions.

Doug: Most organizations that host an event have

to work on a wood floor, and when you do that, you end up damaging the floor. No matter what you do, if you compete enough, you end up damaging the floor. You drop screws and nuts that scratch the floor when you step on them – or gouge the floor when you roll over them with a robot cart. You put tape down that pulls up paint lines from the floor. Using a wood floor for robotics necessitates a lot of repair work.

Mike: In spite of a lot of work to prevent damage, like dropping tarps or plywood to protect it during competitions.

Doug: As we were working to plan this facility , there was A LOT of conversation about the floor and we finally got to the decision that it probably was better not to have to do floor repair every year. The cement floor was a big deal; it took a long time to get resolved. It was a hard decision for everyone because most people don't build school facilities with polished concrete floors. In our case, it was one of those defining moments that really made it easier to host events and cheaper in the long term to maintain the facility.

Doug: What other features of this facility do you think about?

Mike: Another somewhat unique feature of this facility are the blackout shades that we can lower and raise with the flip of a switch. That's important when you've got robots with sensors that are sensitive to light levels. If we have a lighting problem because of sunlight coming in through the windows, we can always close the shades.

Doug: I remember setting up for a regional LEGO League tournament at Grandville Middle School a number of years ago. That facility had south–facing windows at the top of the stands in the gym. We went in there with a set of ladders, and we hung big cloth curtains over those windows as we set up for an event. Elementary LEGO League robots are fully autonomous and they use light and color sensors. Sunlight coming in through those windows would make it impossible for robots to be successful with their standard programming.

Mike: Another thing people don't think about – and we ran into problems with it in our former facility – is dealing with sound. Turns out when you are in a large space with flat walls, every sound becomes an echo. When you bring in 30 or 40 or 100 kids and they work and compete with robots, you can't hear what's going on. In the old facility, we had to hang acoustic panels on the walls to absorb the sound and deaden the echoes. In this building, sound absorption is built in.

Doug: In fact, one of our former Robodawgs was a Boy Scout and did an Eagle project installing sound abatement in the old robotics center a long time ago. Moving into this new building, we knew sound would be an issue. The new Competition Center has sound absorbing panels on the walls and also has a special ceiling with perforations designed to absorb sound. It's very unusual. You can stand in the middle of the arena, which is almost 300 feet long, with hard surfaces all the way around, and sound doesn't echo. It is an amazingly quiet area, given its size.

Doug: We put power in the floors! What a difference that makes. At every event we used to set up, we would have to string out long power runs – long cords with power boxes every ten feet – and we'd spread them out and tape them to the floor. You'd supply 100 pits with 100 power boxes by laying out 500 feet of extension cord with these boxes on it and taping it to the floor so people wouldn't trip on it. In the new building, we put power blocks in the floor every ten feet. Each one has eight outlets in it, and each pair of outlets is on its own 20-amp breaker. That gives us four 20-amp breakers for every ten feet of pit space. That means that when a team trips a breaker, the next pit over doesn't go dark. The power in our floors allowed us to host a middle school State Championship during 2024 where there was only one spot in the entire building where a cord ran across an aisleway. Everything else had the power drawn directly from beneath the pits through those boxes in the floor.

Mike: A beautiful thing. Air handling is also different in this new building. We have been to many drone competitions – even Championships – where air coming from the HVAC system interfered with the flight paths of aerial drones. The Competition Center has an air-handling system that delivers warm or cold air into the building through large bladders with very small holes. Large ceiling fans typically assist this system with air distribution. When the large ceiling fans are turned off, however, you eliminate drafts that could change the course of a drone in a competition. When you set up for a competition, you can fly a paper airplane right through the middle of this facility and its path will not be impacted by air currents. This is a big deal when programming and flying the small, simple drones that our younger students compete with.

Mike: Speaking of drones, we also have a mezzanine above our robot workshop with bleachers for 250 spectators. This overlooks a drone-competition space. There is a net we can pull across that viewing area so that the crowd can watch the drone competition without risk of injury from a stray drone. This is a somewhat unique solution to address safety at drone events – net the audience rather than fly the drones in a netted enclosure.

Doug: There are also 100 seats in that area below the mezzanine that are mobile. It's a mobile set of bleachers we can move anywhere we want. Something else the team got right in this building: the main arena is split in two halves. There's the west half with a cement floor and the east half with a wood floor. They can be used for different things at the same time – or we can open up the curtain in the center and use the entire arena for a robotics event. There is seating there for almost 1,800 people on the north side, another 400 on the south side. It seats just over 2,200 people in the main arena without portable bleachers. With the protected seating on the mezzanine, the portable bleachers, and the fixed bleachers on the north and south side of both ends of the arena, spectators can attend one large event – or several smaller events happening at the same time – without needing to bring in additional seating.

Mike: Another feature in the new building is the new FRC build space. We've got a single build space for all three teams, and it's also used for VEX. You can get to it via two large garage doors. There's no problem moving robots from one place to another. You've got a single FRC build space, so that you can always see what all the kids are doing. From an educational standpoint, and a safety standpoint, it's far superior to what we had before.

Doug: We also have a dedicated machine room now for our CNC machine, our saws, and our drill presses. Next to it, there is a digital fabrication room with our laser cutter and our 3D printers. All of that stuff has a home now behind locked doors for security and safety. Also, the build space has 80 feet of floor to ceiling cabinets. We mentioned earlier there were no cabinets when we originally moved in, but they got them built by Christmas, 2023. Now, almost all our FRC and VEX parts are stored in permanent cabinetry along that wall. It holds hundreds of totes that allow us to keep things stored in locked cabinets inside a workshop, which can be sealed off from the rest of the space. Our favorite special feature may very well be the lockers made to store VEX robots. We've always struggled with how to secure VEX robots and computers when teams aren't there. As part of this building project, they made us 24 lockers sized for a team's VEX robot and computer. The lockers are three feet wide, two feet high and two feet deep – and they all lock. This big locker bank allows us to secure the VEX robots when the kids aren't working on them. That was a substantial change from the old building. In the past, we just set them on shelves in a room and hoped nobody messed with them.

Mike: This new building also has big Mr. Chicklon doors. We have big, overhead garage doors coming from the driveway outside into each of the two competition areas. These make robot load-in so much easier – we have loaded in more than 75 teams in under an hour. It is also amazing to pull a trailer into the building during a winter snow-storm and load up for travel to an FRC event in the warmth of our build space. Or to pull a trailer in on a 90-degree June day and load up VEX parts and fields for summer camp in air-conditioned comfort.

Mike: This new facility has been life-changing.

Moving in may have been arduous, but it turned out to be the calm before the storm. We moved all our stuff into the new facility during July of 2023, but we weren't ready to be in the building yet. We didn't have an occupancy permit. We couldn't really do anything. Our first real day in the facility was August 15 of 2023. That day, we had an open house for the public. We had a ribbon-cutting for the building. It was exciting. (At that time, we did not know that we were just about a year from having the facility fully completed. The final construction task – completion of the Competition Center's video sign on the west end of the building – was done in August, 2024.)

On August 16, we had our second event in the building – our first legislative day. We invited Michigan senators and representatives to come in and see the facility and understand what competitive robotics does in a school setting. It was a really fun day. We had a chance to give them a tour of the building, to show them various types of robots and robot programs. We had lunch with them and talked about how robotics benefits school kids. We think it's really valuable for teams to do these kind of things. In Michigan, we have a state grant program that supports competitive robotics teams in schools. This 99h grant program provides our teams with about $100,000 a year in funding. It's important that our legislators understand the value of competitive robotics programs and continue to support that part of the state budget.

There was a quiet period after we did those open houses. We began to build and practice with our VEX teams, but the facility was still not really ready for us. Contractors were still working in the building every day. None of our storage areas were fully complete. One of the most aggravating problems was the fact that the building had cardkey access on every internal and external door – and that most of the readers on the doors did not work reliably for a couple months after school started. Some days, we were locked out of the building, some days we could not get into the workshop or the fabrication space, and some days we could not get into the bathroom…

October brought our first real competitions in the new

building. We began on October 11 with Mega League nights. Again this year, we ran the VEX Mega League in collaboration with programs in Caledonia, Jenison, and Hudsonville. More than 100 teams from more than a dozen area schools played on weeknights from October to December in this large VEX league. Our first Saturday event, the annual Halloween VEX tournament, was held on the October 28. That weekend, while we ran this local event, some of our teams also traveled to Kentucky to play in the Haunted Halloween VEX Signature event. It was the first of our signature events for the year and our teams had a great time traveling to play against top teams from around the country.

After Halloween, we really began to pick up the pace. The first week of November, Mike and Doug were in Texas helping run the first Bell AVR event of the year. Meanwhile, back in Grandville, we were hosting the VEX Turkey Trot. It had become normal to start our VEX competition season with a Halloween event and a second event the week right after that. This year, with the challenges of a new building, it was harder to run both of these events.

> **Doug:** Mike, I think this is the point where you and I were really starting to feel the pain of the new building.
>
> **Mike:** Yes. I think there were quite a few times where we were thankful for this wonderful building, but it was taking a lot of time getting it ready for actual use. I think that's the point when I coined the phrase: "Nothing works and everything's a battle."
>
> **Doug:** It was. You and I were putting together a Bell AVR field in Dallas, Texas, and it was late in

the afternoon. We were both talking about how hard it was, how we really wanted this building, and how big a deal this was, but we really didn't realize what we were getting ourselves into. You don't realize how big a change this is until you're in the middle of it. We were both talking about being really tired of robotics, and tired of the program, and tired of the kids, and tired of everything. Then you said to me, "Well, Doug, we need to get some shirts that say, 'nothing works and everything's a battle'." Indeed, that's what it felt like at that point in the year. So many things about the new building didn't work. Remember the first time we had an event there and all the men's bathroom backed up all over the floor because the drains didn't work?

Mike: Oh my, yes...

Doug: Remember, we couldn't get into the kitchen area to get a cup of coffee because the electronic lock on the kitchen door didn't work for two months.

Mike: The electronic locks on many doors decided to stop working on us on and off intermittently throughout the first few months.

Doug: We had issues with robots connecting to the fields in every Mega League night in October, and at both of our first Saturday tournaments. We couldn't figure out what that was all about until mid-November as we were running out of ideas as to why VEX robots were subject to so much interference in this brand-new building. When we did the specifications for the building, we had talked about the fact that there could not be anything in this space operating in the 2.4 GHz radio band. As it turned out, someone ordering door locks missed this requirement, and every electronic lock in this brand-new building had a wireless lock operating in the 2.4 GHz band.

Mike: We had been having trouble with those locks, and the contractor thought something must be interfering with them. Their answer was to keep putting up more wireless access points for the lock system.

Doug: They put up more access points so the locks would work better, but the access points and the locks interfered with all of our VEX networks our VEX robots. We were interfering with their system and they were upping their game, putting more hardware in, and it wasn't solving anything.

Mike: Yes. We didn't know we were battling ourselves.

Doug: When we say nothing worked, it was things like that. No one knew why nothing was working with any of the electronics, but we were having a terrible time with our VEX fields and our VEX competitions. We were having a terrible time with the locks in the rooms.

Mike: We can laugh now, but it was frustrating at the time.

Doug: Let's get back to the robotics competitions in November

We're in November. The first weekend, we have the Bell AVR event in Texas where Mike and I are talking about nothing working, everything being battle, and at the same time, they're having a VEX Turkey Trot event in the new building. They had lots of issues that day with the fields dropping connections, and it was the week after that event that we discovered the problem with the locks.

We had some other fun experiences that November. We ran our first Bell AVR events in the new building. Bell AVR drones fly in a giant cage. The cage is 40' long and 20' high and 20' wide. Inside the cage is a 40'x20' wooden field with around a dozen buildings, a water reservoir, a fire station, and a ten-foot river. We put one of those cages up the first week of November so we could run Bell AVR events the second and third weekend of November.

> **Doug:** Hey, Mike, do you remember the day I said, "Hey, Mike, the buildings are on fire?"
>
> **Mike:** I don't think I was there for that particular event, but the buildings in the Bell game were supposed to be on fire. That was the whole idea of the game, that the drones were carrying these marbles, which were supposed to be water, and it carried a laser, which was supposed to be a fire hose. Yes, the buildings were supposed to be on fire, and the drones put them out, right?
>
> **Doug:** That Bell game had ten buildings that "caught on fire," and the drone had to "put the fires out." These buildings were cardboard buildings. They were about three or four feet high and about eighteen inches square. The buildings had warming plates on the outside, so that when you

looked at the building with a camera and looked in the infrared range, you'd see heat and say that building's on fire. The building wasn't really on fire. The warming plate had just gotten warm.

Mike: That's right. It's a simulation.

Doug: The game was designed to be a firefighting game. As we're setting this thing up on the night of November 10 in Grandville, we plugged the field into some floor plugs in the new building that hadn't been used yet. It was late, and some of the team were packing things up. I was working with the electronics, and we turned the field on. There was a pop – and some smoke and flames – and we had a little fire in building six. I said to the guys, "Hey, guys, the field's on fire." They laughed at me and said, "Of course. It's supposed to be on fire, Doug." I said, "No, really." By the time they turned around, buildings 7, 8, 9, and 10 had all popped, and they were all smoking.

We unplugged everything and put the fires out, and we came to find out that there was a floor outlet in the building that had been wired incorrectly. It had been wired with 220 volts and had been that way since we'd moved in. Everything else we had plugged into that outlet on prior days had a switching power supply that could take a 110 or 220 input. The buildings on the Bell field had 110-volt supplies in each building that converted the power for all the electronics in that building – but it was not set up to automatically switch to 220 volts. When we plugged them into 220 volts, it burned out the power supplies. We, indeed, did have real buildings on fire for the Bell competition that year.

Getting back to the year's schedule, November was a really busy month for us. On November 11, we had a Bell AVR event in our building. From the 15th to the 17th, we had teams travel to play in a VEX Signature event at the Indianapolis Motor Speedway. On the 17th, we also held another Bell AVR event in Grandville. On November 18, we ran our annual LEGO League Regional Qualifier. If you think about it, from the 11th to the 18th, we hosted three separate events in the course of a week, all of which had significant setup. This would have been very hard to ever pull off in a gym, but we did it in this new facility. We finished up the LEGO League event, and we had Thanksgiving. On November 28 and 29, we held the Middle School and High School Mega League Championships. These events both ran in the main arena, side-by-side, at the same time those two nights. We had two fields for the Middle School, two fields for the High School, two practice fields, and two skills fields.

The following weekend, we ran our annual Holiday VEX events. These are still our biggest events of the year. That year, they were held while some of our coaches and team members were in Dallas competing at the Bell AVR Championship. On Saturday, December 2, we had VEX U and VEX High School events. On Sunday, December 3, we had our Middle School Holiday VEX event. We had the largest VEX U event of the year that Saturday – alongside an 80-team High School event. The following weekend, we went on to play at Sugar Rush, our next VEX Signature event. It was a great opportunity for our teams to have one last event before Christmas – and a chance for our coaches to take the teams to play at someone else's place, where they set the fields up and they ran the event.

November and December were the most difficult

months of competition in our new facility. We were still figuring the building out, and we were adding new fields with new video and sound.

Doug: Something happened at Christmas that I want to call out, and that is, in this new building, we attracted a different type of donor. Something happens when you go into a facility of this size and do new things that are this visible with this much traffic. You draw the attention of different types of donors who are interested in supporting your teams. Back in April of 2023, our first significant new program sponsor related to the new Competition Center came to us. It was someone that had seen the potential of the new building, and they said, "We want to be part of that." In April of 2023, Bradford White signed a $125,000, five-year agreement to support our high school RoboDawgs and to become the Naming Rights sponsor for our Robotics Fabrication Lab. That was the first sponsorship of this type that we had ever had as a team, and it paved the way for something even bigger to happen December. In December, right around Christmas time, Westwood AI came to us and confirmed they were going to become our second Naming Rights sponsor in the new facility. They wanted to put their name on our competition arena, and they committed a quarter-million dollars to the RoboDawgs – $50,000 a year, for five years. As we wrapped up calendar 2023, we signed this second major, multi-year sponsor – and that began to change the funding model for our teams.

Mike: It did, and correct me if I'm wrong, but I think these were the first sponsors of this type, not just for our program, but for our entire district.

Doug: They are the first Naming Rights sponsors for any facility in our district. To the best of our knowledge, Westwood AI's quarter-million-dollar sponsorship is also the largest Naming Rights sponsorship for any school robotics facility in the country. If you remember, we're the guys that started returning ten-cent cans during the COVID pandemic to raise money for our teams. We still do that by the way, but these new sponsorships opened up new potential for us to equip our building with fields and monitors and things that allow a very different experience for not just the teams, but the spectators who come in the building. We have already grown our programs in both scope and size, but you'll see us really mature multiple new programs during the 2024–2025 school year.

Finally, 2024 arrived.

We started January right at the very beginning. Even before our New Year's VEX event in January, we held a swerve-drive camp at the Competition Center. We have loved swerve drives for many years, but we had never found the time to actually work with a drive system like that before the FRC season started. We now had the space. We found the time. From January 2 to 5, we did a four-day camp. We built three different swerve drives as we started to think about we wanted to build for the FRC season. We built them, programmed them, and had them driving before the first Saturday in January. Which is when, by the way, we held our annual New Year's VEX tournament – and it was the same day that *FIRST* kicked off the FRC season that year. We held our team's FRC kickoff on Sunday, January 7, capping off a busy first week in the new year.

We moved right into FRC build season and, with the move to the new building, our coaches decided to return to some old habits that had served us well. All three of our FRC teams built in the same room, during the same hours each day. We constrained the build hours, challenging our captains to work smarter and to keep every team member busy. We are firm believers in student-designed, student-built, student-programmed, student-tested, and student-run robots. We were more focused during this build season, working no more than five hours on three or four days each week. We're not sure what had the greatest impact on our teams this year, but we fielded the best FRC teams we ever had. Was it getting back to building in one room, with all the teams getting the benefit of each other's experience? Was it the luxury of having a full FRC field built and available every day? Was it the CNC machining, the new laser cutter and the new, more advanced 3D printers in our new fabrication space that allowed for rapid prototyping and custom-part production? Was it the constrained schedule, which kept everyone focused and more productive? Was it finally having fully-experienced seniors after coming off the two years when *FIRST* shut down during the COVID pandemic? We'll never know for sure, but these factors came together to give us really good FRC teams.

Other events in the new Competition Center did not stop just because we were in the FRC build season. We ran

VEX IQ League nights throughout January and February. We ran a late season niddle school VEX event on a Saturday in January – at the same time we had high school FRC teams building and testing their robots in another area of the Competition Center. The RECF Aerial Drone season kicked off in January for our middle school teams and we ran RECF Aerial Drone events in both February and March.

We worked with Jenison and Hudsonville to host the Middle School VEX State Championship at our Competition Center on February 16 and 17 that year. That event brought together 60 of the top VEX teams in the State of Michigan. It was a great event, and we used our entire arena and the related spaces to host the teams. It was our first event running 12 VEX fields – and we believe it was the only event in Michigan to run 12 VEX fields that year. The next day (right after the Middle School State Championship), we ran our first multi-GP drone-racing event in the Competition Center. Teams came from all over Michigan to attend one of the few indoor drone-racing events in the state. We were very fortunate to have some excellent racers in the Grand Rapids area who had been working with us. This first event drew a large number of spectators. Interest in racing led us to purchase the equipment and implement a full drone-racing program for our middle school and high school kids.

The following weekend, we were off to the High School State VEX Championship. Our VEX teams once again won the Michigan High School State Championship. This was our sixth victory in eight years, putting us among the most accomplished VEX teams in the country. On February 27, fresh from the VEX Championship, we headed to Victoria (British Columbia) for our first FRC event of the year. We played in Victoria from February 27 to March 4. This was our third year competing in Victoria, and we were once again part of the winning alliance.

We returned to Michigan – and then headed right back to Canada from March 13–17. We played at the Georgian College event in Barrie, Ontario. The weekend after that, we played close to home, at Grand Valley State University. We then had our last FRC event of the year, from March 28–30 at Kentwood High School. We did well enough at those two Michigan events that one of our teams qualified for the State Championship. This extended our FRC season and we played at the Championship the next week, in Saginaw. This was the first time in 10 years we had qualified a team for the FRC State Championship.

> **Mike:** I think it speaks to the level of play. In this new facility, something happened. We began to see our teams play at a different level. We had a new robot build area, which incorporated all three teams, and something changed. We're not sure we can put our finger on it, but that year, all three of our robots came out of the crate in Victoria, ready to play the game.

> **Doug:** With all the teams in one space, they had a lot more interaction with each other and a lot more support from our coaching staff because you could see all the teams in one place. Thanks to Donors Choose, we also had new equipment. We had new Bambu 3D printers. We had a new laser cutter, which allowed our teams to rapidly prototype and make parts.

> **Mike:** The laser cutter got a lot of use. There were plates on these robots, which held rollers and oth-

er equipment used to collect and lift game pieces. We went through quite a bit of acrylic trying to figure out exactly what shape they needed to be.

Doug: It was probably our strongest set of FRC teams ever. We also saw our VEX teams do very well in the new facility. Our Grandville high school and middle school VEX teams accumulated more Event Champion, Robot Skills Champion, Excellence Award, Amaze Award Award, Build Award, Design Award, and Create Award trophies. In total, by the end of the 2023–2024 competition season, our program had accumulated more than 800 VEX trophies.

Mike: I did not know that. It is an amazing number!

Doug: Now we had to build a big trophy case...

Moving on from the High School State FRC Championship, we headed to Texas for VEX Worlds. VEX Worlds was in Dallas, Texas that year, from April 24–28. Once again, our teams went and played well.

The real story of the Spring, though, belongs to VEX AI. We had played VEX AI during the COVID years. We were the champions at the final Championship event in Texas in 2020. VEX AI was not played in North America from 2021–2023, but it was reborn in 2024

Doug: VEX AI is very challenging for a high school robotics team. It requires the team to build two robots, and for those robots to play fully autonomously, with no human help or interaction. We held our first VEX AI event on May 18 here in Grandville. We went on after that to the VEX World Championship in June. VEX AI really showed us something different this year. We learned a lot about what kids are capable of.

Mike: Yes, we did. You really took the wheel when it came to VEX AI, setting clear expectations for the team and then giving them the resources they needed. We got out of their way and let them figure things out. They had to solve things like: What does each of these robots need to do? How are we going to get these robots to talk to each other? How are we going to develop a winning strategy?

What was really impressive to me was how the kids performed at the Championship. Our teams were able to change their programming on the fly, adapting their code between matches to meet the challenges they were facing on the field.

Doug: It's really an unusual thing for kids to compete with fully autonomous robots. Since they had been in elementary school, they had been using joysticks to drive their robots. Some teams never get past this stage of development – in fact, every FRC robot in the world is driven by students with joysticks. We have really liked VEX AI because there are no joysticks. The robot has to be fully programmed. That introduces a different type of game strategy when your robots play against other people's robots and all you can do is stand back and watch. I think our new facility had a big impact on the evolution of our teams to become

World Champions. We set up AI fields and had the room to work on multiple fields, with multiple robots, every day in the two weeks leading up to the World Championship.

Mike: For us, that meant checking in on where the teams stood with their robots, giving them some coaching, and as you said, getting out of their way. Neither of us wrote any code for those robots, neither of us put any part on these robots. These kids learned how to build two robots that play side-by-side, and to give those robots awareness of where they were on the field. They also programmed multiple cameras to give the robots visibility to field and game elements.

Doug: They were able to use the robots' sensors to know where they were on the field, how they were oriented, and where the game pieces were in relation to them. Our kids did things I've never seen our kids do as they sat and figured out how to code robots to play this game. Let's jump to the Championship. We showed up, and after the first round of the qualification rounds, we were ranked 1, 2, and 3. When we finished 10 rounds of qualification, we were still ranked 1, 2, and 3. Our three teams had started out on top and they remained on top all the way through an event playing against teams that were the best in the world.

Mike: What makes the win more astounding was that our kids played against some college teams. At least one team had a PhD candidate developing and programming the robots that competed against our kids, and our kids won!

Doug: I think one of the things that was really special about our performance at Worlds was how the teams adapted between every match. These kids were off to the practice fields and rewriting code because, when your two autonomous robots play against someone else's two autonomous robots, everybody else is taking notes. They're all watching what your robot does, and they're saying, "If they do that, we've got to program our robot to play against that." You have to stay one step ahead of your competition. It worked out that way. It was a remarkable event. Our kids did amazing things, and they're World Champions.

Mike: Yes, they are.

Also in May, we began our first foray into Combat Robotics in Grandville. The new facility gave us an opportunity to try something new. We began to build combat robots with second, third, fourth, fifth, sixth, and seventh graders. We did elementary and middle school combat robotics in the month of May and June. We had 28 elementary and middle school combat robots. They came to our combat cages at the Competition Center on May 31 to fight for the first time. That evening, they battled to the finish. We were shocked by how many people showed up to watch. The stands were full.

The kids just loved to take a robot and go beat on someone else's robot. We were excited to see how much they learned about building a robot that can turn itself back right-side up, that can withstand a little bit of conflict, and that has electronics and parts that are put in place so they don't fall out when you get hit.

We had our first open-class robot combat event on June 1 – our first Midwest Robot Rumble. We had almost a hundred teams from around the country come to play in that first open-class VEX robot combat event. We operated under the umbrella of the Midwest Robot Combat Association, and all of our qualification rounds counted toward the national rankings of the robots that competed. To say that we learned a lot from that first event would be an understatement. We are so thankful for the wonderful community of combat robot builders that helped us through our first event.

> **Doug:** There is something we need to talk about as we wrap our review of the 2023–2024 year. I think this new facility really caused us to explore new ways to hold more types of robotics competitions. Back when the voters approved this, one of the things we talked about was making sure that we utilized this investment well. During our first year, more than 21,000 unique visitors came through the facility. We hosted more events and more types of events than Grandville ever had in the past. No district that we know of hosted as many types of robotics competitions. No one, short of the World Championship, hosted bigger VEX robotics competitions. No other school district hosted Bell AVR competitions – all the other locations were on college campuses. No school district in the country had a bigger Robot Combat program. This new facility really generated explosive growth in the number and type of competitions we were able to host.

Mike: The facility is definitely well used, and we have a lot for which to be grateful. Grateful to Grandville Public Schools and to the voters who thought this program should be a priority.

Doug: At one point, we were struggling. When everything was a battle and nothing worked. It's interesting to look back on the year and to have gotten through this very busy first year and to really take a moment to reflect on what we have. You and I were talking at camp about how grateful we are for this opportunity. This really was a once-in-a-lifetime chance to build a building like this. We got a chance to do something that most people never get a chance to do. It created so many opportunities for us in the first year, and we can see it opening up even more doors for us going forward.

IT'S NOT ABOUT THE ROBOT!

There are a variety of reasons the RoboDawgs program has proved so consistently successful over so many years. The primary reason is having the right principles and the right priorities for our program. Too many activities for our kids puts the emphasis on the wrong things, and while that may lead to apparent success in measures like the number of kids involved or the win-loss record, over the long haul it ends up shorting the very students these programs are intended to serve.

That's why the RoboDawgs coaches and volunteers constantly remind themselves of two very important principles: it's not about the robot, and it's not about winning.

The first one – it's not about the robot – can be so difficult to keep front and center, because it's a *robotics program*. Surely then, you might ask, isn't the robot is the center of the activity? Well, in a way it is. Of course, whatever robot project a team is working on becomes the focus of that team, at least for a time. But the point of all that activity isn't to make a robot. It's to make better students, better kids, and eventually, better adults. That focus on the kids keeps teams on the right path when it comes to important considerations like grades, participation, teamwork, and responsibility. It's what drove a lot of what Mike and Doug put into that manifesto nearly sixteen years ago – guiding principles that keep the focus of our program where it belongs.

Similarly, the second point – it's not about winning – can help keep both students and adults from running astray. When winning becomes the primary focus of a program, it can erode the focus on much more important goals. Are you involving all the students in all the right ways so everyone benefits as much as possible from the program? Sports serve as a good example here. Those programs, too, can be a tremendous benefit to students during their school years and beyond, driving a focus on excellence, teamwork, and leadership. But with so much pressure on coaches to win, you also see stars who get most of the benefits from some of those programs rise up rather early on, oftentimes in elementary school, while lesser talents are mere placeholders. In robotics, a single-minded focus on winning can even lead to adults becoming the true center of activity, with students serving as mere "worker bees" for adults who do most of the design work and sometimes a good bit of the fabrication and assembly of the robots. You can certainly create a winning robotics team that way, but at what cost to the students who are supposed to be the center of your efforts?

"The biggest lesson is to be more concerned about the kids' success than the robots' success," said Tom Chicklon. "It would be a failure to win at robotics, but not have a student get into an engineering school they want to attend after high school."

Effective adult leadership has been a key element of the RoboDawgs' success. Doug and Mike by themselves probably wouldn't have been able to create anything nearly as successful as what everyone has done together. They're both parents of students who greatly benefited from the program. But Doug is also a successful corporate manager and businessman, and Mike is an accomplished educator at Grandville High School. They bring very different skills and experiences to the table that, combined, are far more than any one person could deliver. They serve as excellent sounding boards for each other, and oftentimes "pressure relief valves" too. And beyond the two of them are dozens and dozens of other very skilled and committed adult volunteers, who have delivered tremendously for our program over the years. The RoboDawgs have a core group of people who've been willing to remain as leaders for a good many years, to provide consistency and committed adherence to the guiding principles, combined with the larger group, who have rotated more frequently but have been no less committed to making it work. They have all been a central element of the program's success.

> **Mike:** One of the aspects that has worked particularly well in Grandville is that the two torchbearers came at this from different directions. Doug is a member of the community, a businessman. He's got lots of experience in dealing with organizations and making them better. I'm a teacher, so I have some knowledge and skills surrounding the school district, teaching and physics. The two of us made a good combination, because together we can walk that line between being part of the school district and being something outside the school district and part of the community.

It takes a number of different kinds of leaders. Adults who haven't been assigned to the program, and who aren't there just for their own kids. It takes adults who see the purpose, who accept they might even sometimes look stupid, and who accept the significant time commitment of eight to ten hours a week. Their reward is getting to know the kids in the program extremely well, and positively effecting their lives in ways they couldn't do in other settings.

To succeed with both points mentioned above, it's also crucial to commit to the basic value that it's the kids who do the work. The kids' hands are the ones on the robots, not the adults'. "If you look at our robots, it's very clear we tell the kids to do the work versus programs where engineers design and build the robots," said Chicklon. "We were somewhat hands-on in the early years, because we didn't know any better. Now we might tell kids, 'I don't think that's going to work, but I've been wrong before.' We allow kids to fail – although we do make sure they don't waste too much time or too much material."

The adults are not shop teachers, and they're not garage mechanics. It's important that they're not interested in designing, building, or programming robots. Instead, they're interested in teaching advanced concepts to kids who want to learn and apply them, while providing support and guidance so they can develop and succeed to the very best of their abilities.

To that point, it's also important that students leave all their labels behind when they enter the Robotics Center. It's unfortunate today that we feel so compelled to hang so many limiting labels on our kids. That's not to say that the RoboDawgs advocate ignoring differences and the special needs that some students may have to succeed in school and life. But when those labels become pre-ordaining, when they provide an excuse for a kid not even to try, that's a huge problem, and one that the RoboDawgs program won't tolerate. In a later chapter, you'll read the story of a particular student that will further illustrate this point, but for now, it's important to know that all of the kids on the program must meet the same basic expectations to participate. The program provides tremendous help and support, but in the end, it's up to each individual student to deliver on those expectations, with no exceptions.

It's equally important that the RoboDawgs are *of* the school but *separate from* the school. Mike and Doug are fond of saying, very plainly, that they can say things, do things, and demands things of the students that it would be impossible for the school to say, do, or demand. Whether it's requiring our students to maintain a minimum C+ average in every one of their classes or requiring that every kid rotate to do every job on a robotics team, they have the flexibility to maintain very high expectations of students that a school-sponsored program simply couldn't. They don't expect them to do all that without help. The program provides mentoring and tutoring for the kids as needed. The coaches keep track of their grades, and work with them to keep them on track with all expectations. For them, it's not just about having the students succeed in robotics, but also helping them to go on and have a successful and interesting life.

"The story that isn't told is the story of the mentors," said BEST's Michael Steiner. "51% of the success of these programs is because of the mentors. The students are the ones who *succeed*, and the mentors are the engine, the inspiration, that enable success."

"It's truly a community program," Bearup said. "There are parents, teachers, businesspeople with kids in the program – and businesspeople without kids in the program. It has its connection to the schools, but it's separate. I would say it's the one program where I don't have to question whether it's the right thing to do, or whether it's doing the right things. And that's coming from a former three-sport athlete, but I don't think I've ever seen another program that does so much preparation for life."

That leads us to the right priorities.

Students must be successful in school

The first and most important of the RoboDawgs priorities is to have every student involved meet minimum grade requirements. Early on, that was one of the more controversial elements of the program. Dating back to the 2008 manifesto, it was intended to ensure students' involvement in robotics – with the time and energy that takes – didn't cause their grades to drop. That would have been counterproductive, since grades are such an important element to determine future opportunities when students are looking at colleges. That drove the decision that the RoboDawg standards would include a minimum C+ grade in every class, as well as a minimum 3.25 GPA in each student's core classes – the ones colleges care most about. Early on, some people were critical of the requirement and claimed it made the program "elitist." But over time, as the RoboDawgs welcomed students from all levels of academic achievement and ability, they were all able to prove those standards were achievable by all the kids.

What's more, when students fall short of those expectations, they aren't just sent away. The program provides a variety of support and coaching, such as a teacher-proctored study hall four times a week, or tutors from a nearby university. Students can remain on the team so long as they're showing effort and progress. However, they might not be allowed certain privileges, such as traveling with the team for competitions, until the grade standard is met.

> **Doug:** One young man came to us as a special-ed student. People didn't really expect a whole lot from him. Being a special-ed student, he got some special accommodations. He was not very interested in doing well at school, but he was very interested in joining the robotics team. Over the first few years he was with us, we worked on his grades, we counseled him, we cajoled him to do better, but we always met with resistance. One year, we had the chance to go to Calgary, Canada, and to to go to the Olympic Oval and visit Banff. Unfortunately, this student's grades were not at a level where we could let him go. We support our kids, and if they're trying hard, we work with them. But we just weren't seeing it with this young man. We informed him that he wouldn't be able to travel with us to Calgary. That raised the ire of both him and his mother. They came in and complained about our grade system, our standards, and the fact that he was a special-ed student and should get special accommodations. We refused. We went on the trip and had a wonderful time. When we came back, this student informed us that he would never again miss a trip because of grades. He'd heard about everything that had happened on the trip, and decided he could never allow that to happen again. He brought in his organizers and notebooks, sat down in our study hall, and got the help he needed to raise his grades.

The following year, we had a similar trip, and he earned the right to go on that one. He did things he had never done academically before. When he graduated, he was accepted to a couple of colleges, but chose instead to join the Navy, where he went on the engineering track and received a succession of training programs. In order to move on from each, he had to be in the top 10% of his class. Each time, he did that. Now he's stationed on a ship in Japan, doing exactly what he wants to do. His mom has forgiven us for imposing such strict standards on him. She's with us at almost every competition. At every tournament we put on, she's there with food and support for us. She can't say enough about the program.

Students learn to work as a team

The program goal for how the RoboDawgs students work together is to do so in a spirit of gracious professionalism. That concept was first introduced in *FIRST* Robotics by Woodie Flowers, one of the program founders and a professor at the Massachusetts Institute of Technology. The concept says that you should play and compete to the very best of your efforts – and that you should also help and support those around you. Obviously, that includes your own teammates. And it also includes other teams, whose members you should also assist so they can play to their highest level as well. That can mean anything from simple moral support all the way to active involvement in helping those other teams have their robots fully functioning and on the field, ready to compete, and to compete well.

Bright students often struggle with teamwork. Within the RoboDawgs, every student is part of three or four different teams each year. That could include a VEX team in the fall, an FRC team in the winter, and an Underwater Rover team in the spring. They have to learn to perform and do well in each of those different groups to succeed. They will be teamed up with kids who are very different from them, including some they wouldn't normally socialize with in the school setting. Kids routinely complain about not wanting to work with a student they've been teamed with, and they're just as frequently told they have to make it work. In the real world, that's what's going to happen – they'll have to work effectively with all kinds of different people. So that's what they're required to do in the RoboDawgs.

"We focus on the program and not on the individual teams," Chicklon explained. "We build continuity by mixing the kids up, having experienced upperclassmen work with our new kids. That can be hard on the parents, with teams being split up after a couple of years. You have to tell people why. But the whole teamwork aspect is so important because that's how the real world works."

Students develop real-world technical skills

There's been a huge groundswell in recent years about America's need for better technical education and skilled trades training. Robotics programs are going to help fill that need, and the RoboDawgs are out in front when it comes to technology. The last chapter covered the different high-tech shop tools, like CNC machining and 3D printing, which the program has had at its disposal for years now. It's been a basic value of the program since its inception that hands-on use of these technologies is at least as important as the theoretical knowledge the students get in school. Yet it's a reality that many college engineering programs don't allow student access to things like CNC machines until their junior year. That's a wasted opportunity.

The RoboDawgs encourage student use of these technologies, allowing all high school students access. By using advanced machinery and technologies to create what they need to build the best robots they can, students also learn the kind of real-world engineering skills that fulfill this priority. The high-tech equipment the program has been able to provide introduces the students to the kinds of technologies they'll likely see more and more as they advance in their schooling, and eventually, in their careers.

Our teams finish in the top half in most competitions

People are often surprised to learn that the RoboDawgs don't really aim to win every competition they enter. The distinction is this: the aim of the program is to build teams that are *capable* of winning every event. Yet achieving a high place in each competition is only one of our many principles and priorities, and those can often conflict. For example, having the students do all the hands-on work of actually designing, building, programming, and then competing with the robots can be limiting. It's a sad reality that there are competitions where other teams have allowed a professional engineer to do the work, resulting in a high-performing and really beautiful robot. The RoboDawgs don't prioritize beating robots like that.

However, experience has shown that the team can still usually finish in the top half, even in an event like that. And the RoboDawgs principal that the kids do the work means the students also gain the absolute most they can from the experience, even if they don't place in the upper ranks of the event.

That also means competing a lot. The RoboDawgs pull their students away from school about five times each year, for a total of about 20 school days. But with program's longstanding success, proven capabilities, and grade standards, teachers support the program and the students who participate in it.

Have a significant proportion of RoboDawgs students enter a college STEM field

The RoboDawgs program is college-centric by design. One of its central goals is to help students gain admission to the four-year college of their choice, and to encourage STEM fields as good choices for many of them.

As with the skills discussion above, there's also much discussion about the increasing needs our society has for graduates with technical degrees, which puts pressure on our institutions of higher learning to find ways to graduate more and more students from fields like the sciences and engineering. Robotics programs help with these efforts by encouraging students to focus on those subjects throughout their lower-level schooling, throughout much of K-12. By the time students have completed years of involvement in RoboDawgs and approach high school graduation, they will have a great many options open with regard to higher education.

A four-year degree admittedly is not for everybody. The RoboDawgs focus on making sure students don't miss the opportunity to achieve one because they couldn't get into a college. By setting the bar high, the program helps them build the kind of transcript they will need not only to get accepted to the school they want, but also to have open to them the high-tech fields they might want to pursue, and to earn scholarships and other assistance to get them through.

Two distinct philosophies have been applied with different robotics programs. In the first, the program leaders believe that school is crap, and they're going to do better than the school. In the second, the leaders believe the robotics program should supplement what the school does. The RoboDawgs are staunchly committed to the second philosophy. The program aims to help students better understand the theoretical concepts they're learning in school through seeing them applied in the robots they build. In school, they learn about math, then at robotics, they learn what math is for. School teaches them concepts in physics, which they then apply to robot design and construction. It gets kids excited about learning because they can use that learning to be better at robotics.

It's also important that we're a program, not an after-school activity or event. There's certainly nothing wrong with those other activities – in fact, they're an important part of a student's development too. But activities and events are usually static and unchanging. That can be fine for other pursuits, but it's simply the wrong way to go about it for a robotics program. Too many things never change and never grow, but there is no way for a long-lived robotics program to remain stagnant, if only because the technologies involved are changing so incredibly quickly. Our students have gone from working on very simple machines controlled with joysticks back in the very beginning to now designing, building, and programming completely autonomous flying machines.

A program that tried to stay the same through that kind of radical change would have failed long ago. To succeed, a robotics program must be one of continuous improvement that constantly builds upon itself.

> **Doug:** When starting down this path, you can begin with a team, or you can start a program. Many people get started in robotics by starting a team. They start an FRC team at a high school to play *FIRST* Robotics. They start a LEGO League team at an elementary school to give their daughter a team to be a part of. They start a VEX team at a middle school so their son and his friends can build robots.

> **Mike:** A program mindset is more than a team. In a program, information is carried on from year to year. A program is broader than a team. It provides students with more structure and more continuity as they move through the educational system. It's not dependent on the longevity of one or two people – it outlasts the people involved.

> **Doug:** Many teams come and go. It is very common for a parent to start a team for their student and to gather other kids and play robot for a few years. What often happens, however, is that, when that student moves on to the next grade-level program, that team comes to an end. We had, in the early years of Grandville Robotics programs, a number of teams that operated in a disjointed fashion. There were LEGO League teams at a few elementary schools. There was one FRC team at our high school. That structure went on for the

first ten years of our program because it didn't act like a program – the high school team took on the character of the current coach and was stronger or weaker based on who was in that seat. The elementary teams came and went as parents at different schools got interested in LEGO League and started a team. Then their kids moved on to middle school and that team ended. We have since found success because, from 2008 on, we've treated our teams as part of a program. It's not about any one team and it's not about any one coach. We've built this with the idea that it will last over the longer term, that knowledge is shared across teams, that parts are shared across teams, that students have multiple options, and that teams endure when the coaches move on. These are all features of a program, and if you are going to have a lasting impact on the students in your area, you need to have a program mindset.

The RoboDawgs don't have separate boys' and girls' teams, and that's another important factor in its success – and one that maximizes its positive effect on our kids. In the interest of demonstrating the earlier point about being able to say things the school system can't, let's be frank. Boys by themselves can have short attention spans, get too physical, and in a STEM setting, feel superior to girls. Meanwhile, girls can fight among themselves and be prone to drama. That being said, all our kids – girls and boys alike – have many (and far more) positive attributes too. But unaddressed, those negative tendencies can make our students' future lives far more difficult and challenging. The way a good academics robotics program requires boys and girls to work effectively together, to work under leadership of both the same and opposite sexes, and to acknowledge the abilities of everyone in each team role, is a uniquely effective way to address those negative tendencies. In being required to work together, all our students behave better.

> **Doug:** People talk about rules around behavior between boys and girls, and it's an area that we have worked over the years to manage. We travel with a lot of young adults, and if you aren't attentive, you could have situations arise that you don't want to be in. We have a rule that says, "No boys in a girls' hotel room, and no girls in a boys' hotel room." I look at this rule as a good example of a policy where we have disciplinary rules that would be hard to administer in a school, but in our setting, they are perfect. When you travel with the RoboDawgs, you may not, as a boy, be in a girl's room or, as a girl, be in a boy's room. The consequences of breaking those rules are that we will send you home. We competed in 2018 in Hawaii. It was one of our more distant competitions. During the course of that event, we had a young lady that went into a boy's room. We contacted the parents and sent those two students home from Hawaii. This was not a popular decision with the parents. It was a very clear step in conformance with our rules, and it helped us establish an environment where the students understand that the rules are not guidelines, that there are some rules that are rules.

In many instances in the public school setting, a student who commits an offense gets a warning. That's a consequence that doesn't clearly communicate when a behavior simply cannot happen again. In our environment, our disciplinary rules are clear and the consequences are immediate. This allows us to travel widely with a group of average high school students and not have problems that most people would expect to see occur.

The Coaches, Mentors, Leaders, and Teachers

Finally, it is hard to talk about things that have made the RoboDawgs successful without looking at key people who have helped lead and shape our teams along the way. Mike and Doug have led the overall program since 2008, but hundreds of other coaches and leaders have played important roles. The RoboDawgs program has given out five Lifetime Achievement Awards over the last 25 years, and we would be remiss if we did not call out the incredible contributions these five individuals have made.

Rosemary Hepfer, Doug's wife, has perhaps played the biggest role. Rosemary is a teacher who has spent years in special education and elementary classrooms. She was an active parent in Grandville schools and served many years on school committees, including multiple years as the President of the South Elementary PTC. It was there that she pulled Doug into coaching a LEGO League team with her. The two of them coached LEGO League teams for many years, starting with one South Elementary team in 2005. They organized Grandville's first competitive robotics tournament – a Regional LEGO League Qualifier – in 2010. From this start, Rosemary and Doug went on to help create LEGO League teams in every Grandville elementary school and the middle school. As Doug and Mike took responsibility for all the growing Grandville robotics programs, Rosemary and Chuck Parks anchored the elementary teams. Over the years, as Chuck gravitated toward the high school teams, Rosemary took on overall leadership for all teams serving 2nd–6th-grade students. She has run after-school robotics for these age levels for almost 20 years, taking us from a handful of LEGO League teams serving a few dozen students at four elementary schools to a program which has encompasses multiple levels of *FIRST* LEGO League and VEX IQ, serving around 400 students each year. She has coached successful elementary teams at every level and has recruited and trained hundreds of volunteer coaches. Rosemary is the key reason Grandville has a vibrant elementary robotics program, and without her years of leadership, our high school RoboDawg teams would not have had the pipeline of excited and experienced robotics students that has filled our ranks for almost two decades. Beyond her elementary robotics leadership – and maybe just as importantly – Rosemary has been at Doug's side helping with our programs for older students. She is a highly successful event partner, and has run robotics tournaments at the elementary, middle school, and high school level. She has traveled to events with teams of all ages. She has supported our high school teams traveling to tournaments all over the U.S. and Canada in so many ways. Among her contributions, the high school team and its leaders have been well-fed across so many locations and in so many circumstances.

Chuck Parks was already coaching a LEGO League team when Rosemary and Doug came onto the scene in 2005. Chuck, an electrical engineer, had children at Cummings Elementary and had found he really liked seeing them create and program robots. (Yes, LEGO League robots were fully autonomous from the very start.) He joined Rosemary and Doug – and Tom Chicklon – in an effort to expand and align Grandville's and handful of LEGO League teams into a program with teams at every elementary school. Chuck was an active organizer, recruiting kids and coaches at multiple schools. He was an early trainer of our coaches, running LEGO League training at Central Elementary for all the coaches in the district. He began to work with the high school teams in 2008, but continued to support our LEGO League teams for more than five years after that. Chuck was a great help with our high school RoboDawgs, encouraging students to explore and build highly creative robots for the *FIRST* Robotics Competition. Chuck also was integral to our first autonomous boat races, designing and fabricating electronic control systems that were not commercially available at that time. (Our RoboDawgs started programming and racing fully autonomous boats in our Great American River Race in 2011.)

Tom Chicklon started in LEGO League with his son, Chris. About the time Chris became a high school student, the RoboDawgs began their first year with Doug and Mike. Tom immediately demonstrated an ability to coach and teach that came naturally to him. Tom's technical background as a systems programmer for a large bank gave him the background necessary to help our students code robots that first year. Since then, he has become our lead *FIRST* Robotics coach, helping students understand electronic, mechanical, and pneumatic systems on robots. Tom also spearheaded the RoboDawgs' foray into CNC Milling. He runs the CNC machine and coordinates training every year. Tom's firm, matter of fact, and gentle way of teaching and coaching students makes him the envy of any professional teacher. The students carry a deep respect and love for Mr. Chicklon. Although his son graduated from high school and the program over a decade ago, Tom is still with us. His dedication to the students keeps him returning year after year.

Steve and Katie Clark were parents of two daughters who became leaders in our program. Steve and Katie saw the impact of the program on their own daughters and other students, and immediately wanted to help. Their involvement grew until they became the lead coaches and mentors of our VEX Robotics program. They became "VEX Mom and VEX Dad" to many of our students. They organized our VEX leagues, Mega Leagues, and all of the VEX tournaments we hosted for more than half a decade. At many tournaments, both in and out of Grandville, they were a fixture in black-and-white stripes, refereeing matches. Steve would usually be the head referee. With nearly a perfect recall, he could pretty much site any rule by number on command. This made him an excellent referee to call violations and settle disputes. Again, a love for the students drove this particular couple to dedicate innumerable hours to the program.

WHAT A SUCCESSFUL ROBOTICS PROGRAM DOES FOR KIDS

With a history now spanning many years, the Grandville RoboDawgs program has demonstrated that competitive robotics has a great deal to offer to every student. Programs like Grandville's are constantly touted for their ability to introduce students to STEM concepts and provide hands-on education. As Dean Kamen so artfully described it, robotics is the only competitive school-based program in which every participant can go pro. That's absolutely correct and vitally important in a number of ways.

Successful robotics programs teach hands-on science and math skills. This seems so obvious, but robotics really makes what the students learn in class tangible. On the team, we have the advantage of time and complete engagement of the student. There are so many vivid examples of students really grasping and understanding science and math while working on a robot. One example that really stands out involves the unit circle. In math class, they learned that a unit circle is a circle of radius 1 centered at the origin in the Cartesian coordinate system in the Euclidean plane. Unit-circle math teaches kids how to find the values of trigonometric functions (sine, cosine, and tangent) for any angle. All our students learn about the unit circle in class, but we have found that many don't really grasp what radians are all about until they need to use unit-circle math to accomplish something they care about. The time and pressure of competition create an environment where they suddenly care about the unit circle.

> **Mike:** We first discovered the opportunity to make the unite circle "real" for our teams when we were building and programming autonomous boats. Our boat program was challenging for a variety of reasons, but working through how to use compass headings and GPS information to steer the boat can really stump a team. Unit-circle math was critical when it came to determining the heading the boat needed to travel on to get to a specific destination.

> **Doug:** I remember the first time we were sitting with the team talking about programming their boats to navigate the lakes at Millennium Park. And the excitement when they successfully did math using a unit of measure (radians) that they had never had to apply in any situation before. This was such a powerful experience for me, as a coach, that I still remember exactly where I was sitting when I first saw the light bulbs go on for our team. It happened on an ordinary October afternoon, in the old school cafeteria on Prairie Street.

> **Mike:** There are examples every week where a light bulb goes on for a team member who really understands how a principal of physics applies to

something they are building or testing.

It's hard to overstate the impact of robotics on kids who take what they learn in school and experience it firsthand. Kids learn about center of gravity in physics, then they apply the concept so a robot they're designing is stable and steers well. They learn the impact of speed when the center of gravity is too high. They learn where to place a gyroscope to further stabilize the robot, and how to use counterweights. RoboDawgs students learn things through experimentation – like the fact you need holes in the launching deck for a frisbee to equalize pressure under the disc so it will release properly. By applying theoretical concepts in robotics, kids understand science and technology better because of their tactile experiences. When you use what you've learned in school to solve a problem in the real world, you understand it better.

At the same time, kids learn the limitations of technology too. In using ultrasonic sensors, for example: if you don't use them in the real world, you don't realize all the problems you can have with them. Factors like reflections and range limitations have to be taken into account in the design when you're using them, or the robot fails. We like the fact that, most of the time, kids can't just go Google the answer. The technology is too new, so they have to solve the problems for themselves.

Competitive robotics enhances and reinforces what students learn in the classroom, but they also learn how to work as a team, with a very diverse group of teammates. Most other school programs cater to a narrower band of students. Sports are the most significant extra-curricular activities in many places, but those teams provide limited options for students who aren't gifted athletes. Robotics, done properly, is exactly the opposite, welcoming students of all abilities and interests. The RoboDawgs serve a broader range of students than any other after-school program. There are top-ten academic performers and students with special needs, there athletic students who letter in multiple sports, and kids who can't catch a frisbee. The breadth of the group creates an amazing atmosphere. There are so many stories of kids finding a home on the team. One student, who transferred to Grandville from the Chicago area recently, comes to mind. Upon joining the RoboDawgs, he went home and said, "Mom, I found my people." He had friends he could sit with at lunch in his very first week at Grandville High School.

That inclusivity is even more important when we look at what we think is, perhaps, the biggest benefit of robotics – it puts all students participating on a higher trajectory. If you could plot the line of personal development and accomplishments over their lifetime for each student before and after involvement in robotics, every single line would have a steeper curve in the upward direction because of their time in robotics. A student who previously looked to be on a path to failure might instead have a flat line of constant performance. One who might have been on a fairly flat trajectory would move to a path showing improvement. And one who was already improving over time would increase their rate of improvement. Even the very best students see their abilities and opportunities made even more positive by joining a good robotics team. Many colleges and businesses are actively recruiting graduates who participated in robotics because they've found that those individuals progress at a faster pace than their peers who didn't experience in competitive robotics.

Doug: I remember a young woman who came to us as a freshman was an average student – but a hard worker. Let's call her Lynn (not her real name). She was a very typical freshman girl coming into a program full of experienced kids. Lynn wasn't too expressive in her first several months as she worked to find her place. She became part of an FRC team in her sophomore year that was doing well, but whose captain had a number of scheduling conflicts. Due to her captain's scheduling conflicts, we had times where we had to assign someone else to act as captain. Lynn seemed like the right person. She was dedicated and smart, and she'd been performing very well in school and with the RoboDawgs. We took her into the hall and said, "Well, hey, why don't you be captain today?" Her eyes got as big as saucers, and she mumbled that she didn't know if she could do that. We said, "We're right here. You've got this – and we've got your back. Hop back in there. You know what the team needs to do. Just go help people keep things moving along." Lynn stepped in that day and ended up leading that FRC team. That was the beginning of the leadership roles she had with the RoboDawgs. Lynn led FRC teams each of the following two years, captained her own VEX team, and was known in her senior year as "Mom" to the whole team. She was always organized, she was always someone the other kids could talk to, and she was always looking out for everyone on her team. Lynn's story is particularly memorable to me because I didn't know her parents very well. We learned more about her in her senior year. Her parent were divorced. Her dad was somewhere else in the state and her mom was working in Chicago. She had been at home alone during the week, washing her own clothes, making her own meals, and getting herself to school and to RoboDawgs. We knew some of this but we didn't know how important the program was to her until she graduated. Her parents reached out and said, "Can you come to an open house for her? We want to make sure to schedule it so you and your wife can be here." We went, and during the open house, her parents asked us to step into the kitchen. They proceeded to tell us how important our program was in helping Lynn build confidence, in keeping her focused in school, and building her strength as a leader. It always makes me feel good to hear that.

Mike: The story continued as she went on to Michigan State University. We got a letter from her mother not long ago saying, "I want to let you know how well she's doing at MSU. She just aced all her classes again this past semester. I hope you know how much of a positive influence you and the team had on her and on so many other students at such a critical time. Thank you for believing in her and helping her grow to be the confident young lady she is. I'm fortunate as a parent to be able to see my daughter grow up so much since being in your robotics program. Thank you again for all the program does for GVHS students. We are so lucky to have it."

Part of the improvement students see is because of the competitive nature of the program. With robotics, every participant feels the pressure of competition. Time and pressure create results you don't get without them, so reaching far more students with those challenges is a tremendous benefit. Time and pressure make diamonds, after all, and they make great thing happen in robotics programs too. They create conditions where the participants *care*, even if just for a short time. Kids learn to make and do things they didn't think they could.

Robotics teaches kids how to play fairly and in collaboration with others. To reiterate the point from the earlier chapter on the Grandville program's success, robotics competitions that are handled correctly teach the kids that it's not only about winning. In fact, the robotics-competition programs the RoboDawgs have chosen to be part of emphasize the need for both competition *and* collaboration. Some include a formal element of working in conjunction with other teams, but they all foster an attitude of helping others. It's a real challenge because, as anyone can figure out, if you help opposing teams, that might also help you get beaten. But it also teaches kids how things work in the real world, where competition and cooperation must exist hand in hand. It helps make them a more productive member of society. It's part of that increased trajectory, helping improve what kind of adult they will become. It forces them to compete *and* collaborate effectively with everybody: their own team members and competitors, adult leaders, the opposite sex, and people who might be quite different from them.

Mike: We have students of all different academic abilities: high-functioning honor students, special-ed students, and all academic layers in between. We had one student – let's call him Bob (not his real name) – who came to us with a special-ed background, and we discovered that he was having trouble in school. The main reason was that he had difficulty reading. In fact, we discovered that Bob could barely read at all. We had a number of challenges with this student and did our best to help him work through his academic difficulties. We engaged a tutor to work with him and, in one year, we helped him raise his reading level from second grade to sixth grade.

Mike: I remember an issue we had with Bob when we traveled to a competition across the state. Bob was rooming with another student at our hotel. The other student was younger and very immature, and the two of them decided it would be cool to stack all the furniture on one side of their room. The hotel personnel were not happy about this

Doug: To say they were unhappy would be an understatement. When we found out what they'd done, we took the two of them aside and told them that, as a consequence of their behavior, they were going to need to go into the pits at the event and find ways to help other teams. They found a team that was having trouble with their drivetrain – a rookie team that was really struggling. We lost track of these two for a while, but they kept coming back to us and asking for parts. We were watching teams compete that afternoon, and it was then that we realized they had become de-facto members of the other team. They had helped them get their robot running and wound up on the field wearing the other team's T-shirts. Bob, our special-needs student, had been a huge help to that team. Up to that point, we weren't sure what he was getting from our program, but that day, at that event, things came into focus. It turned out Bob had learned a lot about our robots. He was able to help fix the other team's robot – and he wound up driving it in competition.

Mike: Late that afternoon, I went to talk to the team's coach, and he thanked me up and down, as though it was all my idea. With tears in his eyes he said, "I hope some day my own children will be as amazing as these young men you sent us." I didn't have the heart to tell him that both students had been a discipline problem and we'd sent them out to help other teams as a consequence.

Robotics also challenges kids with the rate at which the technology they work with changes. The amount that the hardware and software in use in robotics programs changes from year to year can be astounding. The RoboDawgs program has focused on challenging the kids with more advanced technology every year, and we have pushed into new areas to challenge our kids. We built our first aerial drones in 2013 and have built and flown drones ever since. (Grandville is the only school around the area without a "no drones" policy. The school board lets the RoboDawgs fly because the team has operating protocols, a safety check- list, and a demonstrated ability to do it safely.) In 2020, our high school team began competing in events that require students to design, build, and program fully autonomous drones, which introduced technology even the coaches did not have experience with. The students had to not only build an air-worthy flying machine, they also had to develop software to keep it in the air, and complete a series of challenges. Today's robotics programs introduce students to the latest that technology has to offer, and they get to experience firsthand new hardware and software advances they otherwise would never be exposed to.

It's not just the rapidly advancing technology itself that kids are learning. Because the teams are often building things from scratch, the students have also had to learn manufacturing technologies. As discussed earlier, the RoboDawgs brought in a CNC machine as a first foray into making parts in a more industrial way. That introduced the kids to machining processes, machine-tool basics, and computer-aided design and G-code. The RoboDawgs program brought in 3D printers before they were even a "thing," buying MakerBot machines when they were still experimental. The coaches gave them to the kids and told them to start designing and printing parts. They were taught to write down the settings any time they found a method that worked. We set up 3D printing room and let kids play with these experimental printers and learn. They had to learn the intricacies of 3D printing – variables like fill rate and its impact on the strength of the finished part. The kids were making parts for robots on the 3D printers years before any school had purchased 3D printers or incorporated them into a classroom. Designing parts for 3D printing also required CAD expertise, so that meant helping the kids learn SOLID-WORKS. Working with CNC machines and 3D printers, the students learned the differences between additive and sub-tractive machining. They had to learn about tool selection, tool pathing, G-code, and even design for manufacturing. In schools at that time, CAD students simply made drawings – they never actually had to make the things they designed. But in the real world, you can actually design things that can't physically be made – the machines can't mill it or print it as it's designed, or if it's multiple components, they may not be physically able to be assembled. That's another area where applying the school concepts in the real world results in much greater overall abilities.

Students learn about more than technology. They learn about repeatability, both with the robot and on the field. The world isn't level, after all, and nothing rolls straight. Robotics makes the butterfly effect, in which a small change in environment can make a big difference in outcomes, very obvious. The world is messy. Lines aren't straight in the real world, unlike in math. Our kids learn about probability too. It's a RoboDawgs mantra that, if you can make some-thing happen ten times in a row, it's likely to be successful in competition. The benefits of trial and error become very apparent. "Robotics lets kids try new things," said Bearup. "Sometimes they'll fail, but then they learn from that failure and expand their knowledge."

The Grandville teams destroy so much stuff, but all with a purpose in mind. Kids learn best when they have the freedom to figure out how to build things themselves. It's a different mindset from the way we do school. You can't tell a teenager anything – sometimes they have to learn it for themselves. In the robotics world, that means they break stuff along the way. That wouldn't be okay in the school environment – but it's a necessity in robotics.

Mike: There was the time the kids built the air-defense system that was made primarily of parts from the Shop-Vac from my garage. One of our teams wanted to use directed air (like that which came out of the back of a Shop-Vac) to defend their robot's trailer from lightweight balls, which other robots were throwing at it. I brought the Shop-Vac in and the kids quickly proved that the airflow could actually deflect the lunar balls that were thrown at it.

Doug: I remember that the kids said, "We think a leaf blower would really be an interesting idea for defense," because that year, the robots were trying to throw balls into the back of the other team's trailers. Our kids said, "One way to defend our trailer is to blow the balls away as they throw them at us." I remember you brought in your Shop-Vac and said, "The top of my Shop-Vac is a leaf blower." Before long, they had taken that thing apart and had put a *FIRST* motor inside it in place of the motor that had come with it. They totally destroyed your Shop-Vac, but they had created this blower thing. Then they found that it didn't have enough air movement to deflect all the balls being thrown. They decided they would get some marine fans and put them in line to accelerate the air coming out of the pile of Shop-Vac parts. They found two of those marine exhaust fans, ripped the motors out of them, and put *FIRST*-compliant motors into them. They went to the competition and, indeed, their "air defense" prevented other teams from successfully shooting balls into their trailer. This caught the eye of the judges, and our team earned the Xerox Creativity Award at that event.

Any discussion about what students learn in robotics has to include the teamwork skills they learn. As pretty much everybody realizes now, it's very difficult to be successful in our world if you're a pure techie. Almost every job out there involves teamwork. Competitive robotics teaches amazing technical abilities, but all within a team setting. As with the real world, you're very unlikely to win without teamwork. An excellent illustration is the time the RoboDawgs were competing in Waterloo, Canada and they discovered that the gearboxes they were using would not allow them to complete the end game of that year's game. (You read the lead-up to this story back in chapter 5.) It was the day before the final competition, and the four replacement gearboxes were sitting at the Robotics Center in Grandville.

> **Doug:** Mr. Parks goes to Federal Express and ships us four gearboxes overnight. We're near Toronto and FedEx has some trouble getting the gearboxes there overnight due to a winter storm. We got a call at 8am on Friday morning that the gearboxes are sitting back at the hotel, at the front desk. That morning, the kids had begun to compete and they decided that, during the day, they were going to take the time to tear the robot apart and replace all four corner gearboxes. It had taken them a week to build these four corners originally, and somehow, with less than an hour available, they were going to tear all four corners apart, replace

the gearboxes, and get back on the field. Looking at the schedule, the kids decided the right time to do it was during the lunch break. That's when the Waterloo miracle occurred. You saw a team of 14 kids gather around the robot and break out those four new gearboxes – then 14 sets of hands go to work. This was a point in time when the kids needed some space to work, and I figured it was better for me to go get some lunch, rather than be in the way. So I grabbed my sandwich and my Coke and said, "I'll be back in an hour. Let's see what you can get done." Off I went to the stands, where I sat and ate my sandwich.

Mike: An hour later, you came back to find that this group of kids had successfully rebuilt the drivetrain of that robot. They had taken all four corners apart and had replaced all four gearboxes, and had the robot back in operating shape. This was no small miracle. You had to have four knowledgeable groups of kids, each working on their corner of the robot, handing tools across the robot and handing parts across the robot, to get it done in that period of time. People often talk about those times when a team begins to gel and the members finally begin to act like a well-oiled machine. This was that moment. And what a team they were after that incredible rebuild. That team won every remaining match that weekend in Waterloo. They went to an event in Troy the next week and won that too. This team advanced to the *FIRST* Championship in St. Louis, and finished fourth in their division. This was a team that struggled in their first two events – and then the Waterloo miracle occurred. I'll never forget that day.

Teamwork goes beyond working well with members of your own team as well. Robotics encourages teamwork *among* teams. The Gracious Professionalism award in *FIRST* Robotics recognizes "cooperitition": putting forth your best effort not only to help your own team, but to help those teams that you're competing against as well. That's a value the RoboDawgs embrace enthusiastically, as evidenced by the many times RoboDawgs teams have won that award.

Doug: A story that comes to mind is from Calgary in 2013. Alongside us, in the pit next to us, is a team from Father Mercredi High School in Fort McMurray, Canada. I use the word "team" lightly, as the only person in the pit was a young man named Herman. We came to refer to him as "Team Herman" because he showed up by himself with a bag of parts. He had started the season as one member of a four-member team, but the other three members had quit just before the event. His coach had got held up as he was leaving for the event, so in comes Herman with his mom and his bag of parts.

Mike: It was literally a bag of parts. He did not have a robot. He had pieces of a robot – stuff they had worked on – but he had nothing to compete with. And here the miracle of *FIRST* appears. This is one of the things we value in *FIRST* that you don't see in other robotic events. That miracle occurred when some of our kids looked up and said, "Let's go help Herman." Off went our kids. Some kids from a team called SWAT came over too, and they went to work with Herman and his bag of parts.

Doug: Most teams spend six weeks building a robot. Over the course of that single day, these kids created a robot. They scavenged parts from our pit and used the parts Herman had brought. As Herman's mom watched, these kids and Herman transformed a pile of parts into a functioning robot.

Mike: Our captains and our most experienced students were working on our robots. The students who went to help Herman were not our top-tier students. They went in there and they created a drivetrain. They helped Herman program it. Those RoboDawgs, along with SWAT, became Herman's team. We saw things out of our students we didn't think we could see.

Doug: It was amazing to watch this bag of parts transformed into a functioning robot before inspection closed that day. Herman was ready to compete with that robot – but in order to do so, he needed a drive team. In *FIRST*, one person can't run the robot alone. So, with embers of our team and SWAT joining him, Herman went to the field and completed.

Mike: One of our parents went out and bought matching T-shirts and we created Team Herman. They wound up in the middle of the pack, 15th out of 29 teams, and were selected to play in the playoffs the next day.

Doug: It was exciting to watch this young man who'd come in wondering why he was there, who gets credit for showing up because sometimes that's half the battle. This kid who had started his season six weeks prior came to an event and saw success in less than three days. That's the miracle of watching *FIRST* work because so many things come together to enable kids to do things you wouldn't believe they could do.

Mentoring is another skill students learn in robotics. Team members benefit from the mentoring of a group of coaches. Coaches in the RoboDawgs program mentor and tutor the kids. They keep track of their grades, helping them to meet our minimum-grade standards. The adult leaders' interest in them goes far beyond the robotics program and far beyond their school career. It's a stated goal of the program to get every one of the students accepted to a good college and have each of them go on to a rewarding career. As the RoboDawgs program has become more and more developed and well-known, more and more colleges, now including Michigan State, Michigan Tech, and Western Michigan University, have begun actively recruiting from the program's ranks. One of the biggest rewards the adult volunteers have from involvement in the RoboDawgs program is tracking the progress of the students in the years after they move on into the bigger world.

It's not just the adults mentoring students, though. The older RoboDawgs mentor the younger ones. Members of a high school RoboDawgs team, for example, will mentor younger students on VEX or LEGO teams. That becomes mutually beneficial, with the older student learning important interpersonal skills like patience and effective communication, and the younger student benefiting from the older one's technical knowledge and greater maturity. The younger students look up to the older ones and are motivated to continue in the program because of that. If you visit west Michigan, you'll find young kids wearing T-shirts emblazoned with the words, "Future RoboDawg." These shirts help create a spark of interest in competitive robotics before kids are even old enough to participate.

That mentoring of younger students, along with our requirement that almost everyone take a turn at being team captain, builds leadership skills. In school, it's easy for students to hide away in a chosen persona, whether that's jock, nerd, super-popular fun kid, or class clown. There are kids who are natural at leadership and others who think they just don't have what it takes. We don't let them hide from leadership, or from any other role on the robotics teams. They're required to take on that front-and-center role, even if they're not comfortable with it.

> **Doug:** Early in one FRC season, we were headed to a competition in Lansing and our captain at the time was unable to attend. The coaches went into this grand debate about who the replacement should be. No candidate clearly jumped out, and we decided to take one of the kids and give him a shot at it. This was a kid we weren't too sure about; who we weren't sure would take it seriously enough to get through the weekend. But he went, and wow, did he do a great job in Lansing!

Mike: Yes, he did. He stepped up. He became the leader. He was no longer the clown of the team. He took the job seriously. He was able to organize the students, and was able to give orders without being a boss. It was one of the first times we saw a student really step up and grow because we gave him the opportunity to do something significant.

Doug: This is one more example where the pressure of time and competition created an environment where a student out-performed everyone's expectations. This young man went on to complete a degree in Computer Engineering at a midwestern university, graduating *magna cum laude*. He spent time as a research assistant at CERN, working with the world's largest hadron collider (in Switzerland). Today, he's a Principal Flight Software Engineer at NASA's Goddard Space Flight Center.

WHAT A SUCCESSFUL ROBOTICS PROGRAM DOES FOR SCHOOLS

Robotics Enhances Traditional Education

Just as robotics can improve a kid's trajectory in life, having a robotics program improves a school system's trajectory too. Regardless of what path the school system was on before robotics came along, a good robotics program will make schools better and better over the years.

Public education, its structure, methods, and outcomes can be a very complex and contentious topic. We have talked to robotics coaches who have nothing good to say about public education. They feel that science and math are taught in a way that is not engaging, and see robotics as a replacement for traditional instruction. After 17 years of coaching competitive robotics at high school level, we see things differently.

Good science teaching can happen in a traditional classroom. Let's take an example from physics education. It starts with an understanding of where your students are, engaging their curiosity, and helping them to begin thinking like scientists. Modeling is one way of doing this. The students are faced with a question or challenge, they go into the lab, perform experiments, and collect data. With some guidance from the teacher, they analyze their data. Then they publish their results digitally or through a whiteboard presentation. The entire class then grapples with the results to find meaning and understanding. This is not engineering, it's science! There are very practical aspects to this, but the main goal it to help students use evidence and reasoning to come to basic conclusions about how the universe works. Public–high school classrooms can do this, and do it very well.

Then comes robotics. The basic concepts of physics can be found everywhere on a competitive robot. Students must apply what they have learned in science and math classes to something ultimately practical. This is not science, it's engineering! This is the use of the discoveries of science to build something useful and fun. Here are just a few examples:

Students realize the uses of radian measure. When a wheel turns so many radians, just multiply that by the radius of the wheel, and we know how far that wheel went down the field. Suddenly, while attempting to create usable code, the students discover the utility of radian measure!

Students realize the uses of mechanical advantage in levers and gear boxes. When attempting to lift a game element that weighs less than a pound, students learn the impracticality of building a long metal arm with heavy motors and manipulators several feet from the pivot point. No matter what gear ratios you can come up with, or how many motors you have available, some good, simple physics is what you need to make your robot's manipulators work well.

In my AP Physics class, students learn that power is

a product of torque and rotational velocity. Suddenly, in robotics, the torque and speed tradeoffs in motors and gear boxes begin to make practical sense.

Our point is not that an after-school robotics program will ever replace STEM education – it does not have the structure or depth to help students understand the multitude of science and math concepts that are required to prepare students for higher education. Robotics, however, does re-inforce these ideas. Robotics makes science and math real, practical and necessary in the minds of students. A robotics program meets needs that cannot be met in a classroom setting. Instead of replacing what happens in the classroom, robotics is additive and enhancing to what takes place during the school day.

What Robotics Does for Teachers

The benefits of a robots program for students are many and varied, but there are some real benefits for teachers who participate in these programs as well. Teaching is a job like no other. High school teachers feel the stress, the responsibility, and the pressure of being accountable for the instruction and wellbeing of 25 to 30 students (when class sizes are reasonable) for 59-minute blocks, five hours per day. There are many who don't see teaching this way. They look at our "five-hour-per-day job" and see it as part-time at best, unworthy of respect. Respectfully, these individuals have never taught. They have never been responsible for multiple lesson plans, lab experiments, assessments- and the never-ending grading. Also, that does not account for the emotional and physical needs of students based on their varied backgrounds and home circumstances. Add to that, the constant meetings and district initiatives that add to the workload and you have a job that goes way beyond what people from the outside of the classroom see.

Now, you are going to ask such a person to meet with students after school, build a robotics program, and become involved in activities that require evenings, weekends, and long stretches away from school – which actually increases, not decreases the workload. In recruiting other teachers to become robotics coaches, we have never disrespected their reasons for saying no. These are not lazy people driven by self-interest – they are, after all, teachers. Some have young families, some are already coaching a club or sport, but the most common reaction that we have noticed to the prospect of coaching robotics is fear.

Teachers are trained to be the masters of their class-rooms. This is especially true at high school level. We know our specialties. When we walk into the room, we are pre-pared. We know what the lesson plan will be, what back-ground knowledge is required, and we can do all the assigned problems on the board. But robotics is not like that. When you are building a robot, drone, or Underwater Rover, you just can't know everything, yet teachers feel that they do need to know everything. This is the source of the fear. In-stead, we are surrounded by people who do have experience in these systems, and we have online resources, and we can figure it out. Students can figure it out. Sometimes the best way is to give the students these same resources and get out of their way! We live in a world in which knowledge doesn't just exist in a book or a teacher's head any longer.

We have to get past that. Students must understand what they don't know, and have the habits of mind to be able to find what they need. This is world in which we now live. We can't be afraid to not know something before our students do.

Added Benefits for Teachers Who Become Robotics Coaches

They have more time with students to build relationships and to understand their lives, and to help them pay attention to grades. This has been a serious benefit for teachers in our program. They see these students for hundreds of hours during the course of the various robotics seasons, much more than would be possible during a traditional six-period day. As icing on the cake, they get to see what these students do after they graduate! Teachers enter this profession to change lives; to help student to achieve their dreams or realize a path they never considered. Robotics helps teachers to fulfill their life mission in a big way!

> **Mike:** When I was a student teacher, my supervising teacher was a former basketball coach. The year I was his student teacher was his last year of teaching before retirement. When I left him to start the search for my first physics teaching position, he gave me some advice. Find some activity, sport, or club that you are passionate about and share that passion with students outside the classroom after school. Building those relationships with students, knowing that you are helping them to grow beyond the classroom, will enhance your career in ways that you cannot calculate. It's the difference between a good career and a great one. I've always tried to take his advice through Science Olympiad and now robotics. It's been a wild ride, but I am very grateful that I can look back on a life well spent.

Teachers who coach robotics have a better understanding of technology and what is possible. Many physics students state engineering as a career goal. Teachers who also coach robotics know what that entails and how the physics they are teaching will help these students in college and beyond. They always have an answer when students ask, "Why do we have to know this?" Demonstrating the relevance of what is being taught improves behavior and motivation.

Robotics gets teachers involved in a different way. It helps get them beyond not wanting to look stupid in front of the kids and gets them connected in a more exploratory relationship. School has a common-core curriculum and all kinds of specific subject-matter requirements. But it doesn't necessarily allow time to do experimentation and learning of new technologies that our program can do. Robotics, on the other hand, gives teachers who are involved in the program an opportunity to affect students much more profoundly than they can just being teachers.

> **Doug:** Having a separate program allows teams to do things for and with the kids that schools can't, and that benefits the students. It benefits the schools too. Robotics programs make public schools better. Kids get to experience in the real world the concepts from school, and they bring that understanding back to their classes, helping everybody in them. Robotics really supplements what the school can do. It's the same as the dif-ference between learning about cooking by read-ing a cookbook versus working in a restaurant. School lab classes can help, but while labs can make some things tangible, such as math, they

struggle with advanced concepts like computer science and programming. For example, if a drone is dropping a ball at the wrong time, students have to understand the underlying code to fix the problem. Schools just don't cover things like that – at least not yet. Robotics makes the purpose of the academic instruction much clearer to the students.

The Future: Changing the Nature of Education

As mentioned in the last chapter, robotics programs make science and technology more tangible for the students. That also ends up helping the schools because those students who apply theoretical concepts they learned in class to real-world problems they're solving in robotics bring their enthusiasm back to the classroom, and become better collaborators with both their fellow students and their teachers. Their classes can only improve as a result.

Robotics also teaches kids other critical concepts not covered in school. They learn to appreciate design and program backups, and version control, for example. It makes education better – it doesn't replace it. The mindset of a teacher is different from the mindset of a robotics coach. A teacher knows things before the kids do, and better than the kids do. That's not always the case in robotics. Students learn to get comfortable learning things on their own.

Schools will change in that regard by sheer necessity. Given technical advancements, including robotics and artificial intelligence, the nature of education will change. But that change will happen slowly. Teaching will also change. But those changes will be driven more from outside the schools than within, and a district robotics program can be a built-in driver of positive change. "We learn a lot in the school system from the things the RoboDawgs do," said Bearup. "We learn new things about what we can do to engage kids better, and better connect with them academically."

Finally, robotics is now also affecting universities. Ever-greater numbers of students are showing up as freshmen in college having participated in robotics for almost their entire school careers to that point. They expect different things from what universities may have offered in the past. "When a student has participated in *FIRST* or VEX or BEST, they're not looking to do a standard university program," said Michael Steiner of BEST Robotics. "They want a buffet, not a fixed menu." Our institutions of higher learning will have to learn to change and adapt to attract those excellent students. When students enter the university with increased capabilities, the university must adapt in order to challenge and meet these students needs. Robotics can be a driver of positive change on all levels.

WHAT A SUCCESSFUL ROBOTICS PROGRAM DOES FOR COMMUNITIES AND BUSINESSES

The positive reach of robotics goes beyond the schools. Competitive robotics programs involve area businesses and community organizations. The most direct engagement of the community and area businesses begins with the funding and operation of the robotics programs themselves. Funding a competitive robotics team can provide positive brand exposure for businesses and organizations that want to be associated with hands-on STEM education. Teams also provide businesses with opportunities to involve their employees with groups of talented students, where they can serve as team coaches and mentors – or as judges or referees at events. The teams, in turn, help students explore and make informed choices from among a wide range of career options. Robotics programs develop future members of the workforce who understand practical problem-solving. Competitive robotics produces graduates with leadership skills, and future employees who have experience working on successful teams made up of people not always like themselves.

Robotics programs, like most extracurricular activities, improve the communities they serve. They do that in a variety of ways. They bring people together, young and old, with a common purpose and healthy organizing principles. They drive regular positive social interactions and foster a sense of belonging for those who participate in any way, whether that's students who are directly involved, parents, teachers, or other adults who volunteer, or simply spectators at shows and competitions.

Academic robotics is one of the best builders of communities among the many different extracurricular activities. Many activities focus only on the immediate areas they serve, so their reach for community-building is necessarily limited. Some involve intense competitions that spawn rivalries with nearby communities, which may be perfectly healthy, but can also drive wedges between the various communities in an area. But because academic robotics programs combine competition with cooperation among teams, they bring people together across large areas – even internationally – much more than activities that focus on pure competition. "It's become one big community in the area," said Tom Chicklon about the effect of robotics on Grandville and its surrounding towns. "We have teams lending us their fields for competitions. To be part of that is something I never would have expected."

"It's truly a community program," added Superintendent Roger Bearup. "There are parents, teachers, businesspeople with kids in the program, and businesspeople without kids, all involved. I would say it's the one program around where I don't have to question if it's the right thing to do, or if it's doing the right things. This might sound funny coming from a three-sport athlete, but I don't think

I've ever seen a program like robotics that does so much to prepare kids for life."

The programs have a very healthy effect on businesses themselves in the community as well. Robotics offers a much richer way for businesses to help support their local schools and students than other programs that simply look for the monetary award of corporate sponsorship. School robotic programs are certainly just as interested in sponsorships from local companies as sports teams and other programs are. After all, robotics played at a high level can be an expensive proposition, involving high-cost parts and materials, program fees, and travel. But robotics also offers companies an avenue for embracing the kind of deeper business purpose beyond simple sponsorship that so many customers and prospective employees are looking for today.

In robotics, businesses – especially those of a technical nature – have an opportunity to support teams with far more than money by directly involving their people as volunteers and mentors. The Grandville RoboDawgs might never have achieved the long-term success they've had without that early involvement of the local company X-Rite when the program was just getting started.

Mike: Natalie Lowell was an engineer at local company called X-Rite. She had seen a robotics tournament at Eastern Michigan University and was just blown away by it. She saw the need for this in public education and in the corporate world, both of which she thought needed to change. She approached her boss and our Superintendent, convincing them both this was something that needed to be done. She got permission for us to go to

X-Rite, and to take the kids into their Research & Development area, which is taboo – you don't let kids go in there! But she was instrumental in making this happen. She was walking the line and keeping peace between all these groups. We had X-Rite's head of R&D helping us, we had a coach from Built on Brains from Holland, Michigan helping, and we had an engineer from Rockwell too. Our first year, X-Rite provided the facilities and the engineering knowhow. That year, it was kind of touch and go whether or not this would work. More than once, the kids made Natalie's head explode, but she was always trying to placate the corporate folks and keep us in there. It was a cool year.

By having their own technical staff support the students firsthand, the company not only helped the team achieve some early successes, but also had its employees showing students what their STEM careers looked like. And today, with the RoboDawgs interacting with the likes of Bell Aviation, their success has opened opportunities for the students to see high-tech applications and careers far afield from Grandville.

Additionally, academic robotics offers businesses a means of directly improving workforce development right in their own neighborhoods. By providing the kinds of support discussed above, companies become direct recruiters for students to give STEM education and careers a look. Their employees, by serving as volunteers, become educators themselves in helping teach young people skills involving everything from the trades to engineering to programming.

With one of the top challenges for companies today being a shortage of employees, especially employees with technical abilities, companies that support robotics are (at least in part) helping train their own talent pool of the future.

Participating in robotics programs during their educational years gives students a chance to experience science and technology in a hands-on environment. Doing this over a series of years helps most students find a path for their future career. Students who participate in middle school and high school robotics programs are nearly twice as likely to be able to articulate a career path as high school juniors as students who have not participated in robotics. This is largely because the problem-solving and creativity involved in robotics provides an environment for students to explore their interests. Some students gravitate toward the very hands-on mechanical portions of robot building. Some students find the science, particularly the physics behind the robot's actions, to be fascinating. Still others find that the organization of a team and the methods for making teams successful get them excited. All of these activities help prepare students for a lifetime as productive members of society.

Perhaps the greatest benefit to businesses is the ability of robotics programs to generate students that pursue a wide range of career interests. Graduates from the Grandville Robotics program go in many directions, and most have a clear sense of where they want to be. Robotics teams bring students of all capability levels and many interests together to work as a team to build a robot. In that environment, students learn what they like and don't like. They learn what they're good at and not good at. Businesses benefit because robotics programs, through this process, produce a wide range of high school graduates that are on different career paths. Many graduates from the Grandville robotics programs move on and pursue an engineering or computer-science degree in college. Others go directly into the trades, pursuing a career as an electrician or a machine builder. Of the kids that go to college, some go on and pursue advanced degrees. There are many PhDs scattered across the U.S. who came out of the Grandville robotics program. This ability to bring together students and create a variety of career paths, allowing students to pursue trades, a four-year college, or an advanced degree, all come from the same robotics teams.

Another area where communities benefit is in the development of problem-solving skills. The evolution of a competitive robot is simply the result of solving a series of problems. The Grandville robotics programs have many specific robotics teams that work through a process of evolution every season. Students design and build a robot and then compete with it. Following the competition, they look at the things that performed well on their robot and the things that didn't. They think about the other robots they saw and the features they liked. Now, the team engages in another round of problem-solving, redesigning their robot and building generation two. This robot competes and the process begins again. The Grandville robotics program at the middle school or high school level believes teams should compete dozens of times during the course of a season, not once or twice. This iterative process for design, build, program, test, compete, all followed by another cycle of design, build, program, test, compete, gives these teams the opportunity to learn how to solve problems and build an increasingly capable machine over a period of time.

The development of problem-solving skills is strongest in programs that are student-centered, such as those coordinated through the Robotics Competition and Education Foundation. The RECF has the most full-developed and consistently applied student-centered policy in all of competitive robotics. Unlike *FIRST*, where adult mentors are allowed to design, build, and even compete on the field with a team's robot, the RECF requires that students do the work. We were among the earliest advocates for student-centered robotics and our experienced helped influence the RECF's student-centered policy. Their student-centered policy is "intended to increase the awareness of the REC Foundation's goal of student-centeredness, and to transparently communicate its expectations to students, mentors, and other program participants to maximize the learning opportunities offered by their competition programs. The overarching mandate is that students should use designs, code, and game strategies that are consistent with their abilities and knowledge, and not have an unfair advantage by using mentors' work. Student learning should always be the first priority with all mentor actions."

Communities also benefit tremendously because robotics teams teach boys and girls to work together side by side. In so many areas of our society, we struggle with the idea of having men and women work as peers. Yet in competitive robotics, the pressure of time and competition brings students together in a way that forces boys and girls to learn to work together as equals. It forges bonds and friendships between students on the basis of mutual respect. It creates instances where boys perform well working under female captains and vice versa. Over the last decade, approximately half of the RoboDawgs' *FIRST* Robotics team captains have been girls. This experience working under the leadership of a female at a younger age helps develop an expectation that any individual can play a leadership role, regardless of gender. Robotics is uniquely suited to level the playing field between boys and girls and create that environment where they can learn to work together as colleagues.

Employers and schools work hard to teach high-performing students the value of bringing a team along, but actual practical experience that high-performing students get from robotics teams brings that message home. The RoboDawgs' very first team was a *FIRST* Robotics Team, and the program has a strong *FIRST* Robotics Competition element today. *FIRST* Robotics Competition robots are large and complex, and no one student or two students can build and operate a robot. *FIRST* Robotics, more than some of the other robotic competitions, drives this significant learning about teamwork and acceptance of others, which will serve students well throughout their careers and their lifetime.

STARTING A COMPETITIVE ROBOTICS PROGRAM IN YOUR SCHOOL OR COMMUNITY

The number-one thing to acknowledge if you want the most successful program possible is that it has to be about the kids, not about the parents or the robots or winning or anything else. Unless a robotics program is designed to provide the best development possible for the students involved, both during their time in robotics and in school, it won't be truly successful.

So far in this book, you've read a lot about the history of the RoboDawgs program. It's important to note that the program has been evolving for more than 26 years. Grandville has helped more than a hundred teams get started as well, so the RoboDawgs coaches know a lot about how new teams are formed and what it takes to make them successful. Whether your school system has no robotics program right now and you want to get one started, or you have an existing program you'd like to improve, there are lessons from the history of the RoboDawgs that you can use to help you along your own path. The RoboDawgs program has been uniquely successful. "It's definitely one of the most amazing programs I've ever encountered in my 34 years in education," said Grandville School Superintendent Roger Bearup.

It didn't get there overnight. It took years of trial and error, consistent effort, building on successes, and picking things up when they didn't work. There are plenty of lessons there that anyone can learn from. But what you decide to build has to be right for your own community.

A very important thing to remember as you think about your own robotics teams is that one size does not fit all. Grandville started with a single FRC team and took many years to grow to where it is today. After running for years as a *FIRST*-only program, the RoboDawgs eventually branched out to participate in other competitions as well. For a program that covers the whole school system, you'll eventually need to engage with multiple robotics organizations. If your goal is to use a single type of competition as a core for the organization of your program, there's nothing wrong with that. You can certainly partner up with one of the successful robotics-competition organizations and build your program around that, and start to see some success in the early years.

Eventually, however, that can become very limiting. To keep your students challenged throughout their academic robotics "careers," you'll likely find that you need the different approaches taken by different organizations, so things don't get stale and the kids learn a variety of technologies. For example, right now, VEX V5 consists of six years of doing same things with same parts. That can work well for students in their earlier years, but how do you keep kids engaged and challenged as they learn more and more? The concept of engaging with multiple robotics-competition organizations can hurt people's feelings because they've gotten very attached to *FIRST* or VEX or BEST, but robotics is a world where you have to change and upgrade or die.

VEX is now a middle school thing. How do you keep technologically advanced high school students engaged with it? You probably don't, and that's why you'll most likely need to add other challenges. It pays to think about how your teams will be set up to inspire kids to join early in elementary school, with thought given to how those early teams then feed the teams in middle school and high school. You should focus on building what will eventually become a fully integrated program that encompasses all the different levels of education.

The RoboDawgs isn't a *FIRST* team and isn't a VEX team. Instead, it's a program that eventually defined its own path and did what worked for the Grandville schools and community. Similarly, you should take the approach that works best for *your* schools and your community. The many different competition programs available all offer their own advantages and drawbacks, but the ability to mix and match gives each school's program complete flexibility in building what works for them. The RoboDawgs even occasionally throw in the "shop teacher's special" – custom challenges of our own making, just to keep the kids challenged with new problems to solve and new technologies to learn. The RoboDawgs' history is what it is because of the path everyone involved in it has chosen. Your program's path may be very different. It depends on what the coaches, the parents, the students, and the schools want.

It's important to think about what you can start and be successful with, and to look at what has a reasonable commitment for the people involved.

There are five key areas to think about:

1. Can you find support from existing organizations;

2. What group of students is interested in robotics;
3. Where will you get financial support for your team;
4. What experienced leaders are available to drive the program;
5. How many other adults will be there to support your efforts.

You should understand what support you have from organizations around you. Many times, school districts will support robotics teams, but sometimes it's an individual school that steps up where teachers and the principal are committed. Sometimes Scout troops support robotic teams. Many teams are built around homeschool groups. If you're going to be successful with your first robotics teams, you really need to understand who's out there that can support you with an organization.

The second thing to understand before you start a team is how many students are interested and what age they are. Do they have any robotics experience? Do they have any computer-science or programming experience? Many schools start with a small group of students in an elementary school who are interested in building a LEGO League robot. Other schools start with middle school students who begin with a VEX program. Both of these are examples where programs started with a group of students and decided to build a robotics team to meet that group's needs.

The third thing to take stock of before you begin is where your team will find financial support. Many times, school districts have funds to support teams. In many states, including Michigan, there are grant programs to support robotics teams in public schools. The majority of robotics teams are started with contributions from parents that fund the initial purchase of a robot and a competition field. Regardless of where you find your financial support, you're going to need some money to support your team.

A somewhat unusual feature of the RoboDawgs is that the program is not pay-to-play, as so many academic robotics programs are. As a result, fundraising is a critical activity in Grandville. But even for programs that charge students to participate, it's very likely that additional fundraising will be required for the various expenses involved, such as robots and parts, shop-tool costs, tournament registration fees, travel expenses, and uniform shirts.

There are various ways the RoboDawgs have raised funds over the years:

- Raise money yourself (the returnable cans covered earlier, for example)
- Corporate sponsorships
- Crowdfunding
- Donations
- Government funding

Those examples are just a few areas to look at as possible sources for funding for your own program.

The fourth thing to understand as you look at what you start with is the number of experienced adult leaders who have the desire and the time to help provide leadership to your program. You know how many people you have that want to be highly committed to help drive the program in its early months and years. You need to understand their experience. The very best robotics coaches often come from a group of adults that are already highly engaged with youth. Many robotics coaches were also Scout leaders. Many were Sunday-school teachers. Regardless of where they come from, you need a core group of experienced adults who can provide leadership to your program. They must have the interest and desire to put time into it, and they must have the time available to commit.

The final thing you should look at as you take stock of the resources you have to begin a program is the number of other adult volunteers who can play a role in your program, but who won't be leaders in it. You should assess the size of that pool of volunteers, as many things require lots of hands.

One adult you absolutely must get on your side is your Superintendent of Schools. While the RoboDawgs are a separate entity from the Grandville schools, the program is still *of* the schools. An academic robotics program, by its nature, is closely intertwined with the school system it supports, so if there's not mutual agreement about the fundamentals from both sides, the program will fail.

> **Doug:** If you've decided what you're going to start and you've found your torchbearers, the next task is to get your superintendent on board. We have found from watching *FIRST* and VEX, and other robotics teams all over the world, that teams do the very best when they're connected with a school system. To be connected to a school system, your torchbearers have to find alignment with that superintendent and get him or her on board so that you have the right relationship with the school district. In our case, the RoboDawgs were founded with the strong support of the superintendent at the time, Duane Sheldon. He encouraged teachers to get involved and he helped support that original team. Moving through time, another superintendent, Ron Caniff, came through our district, and was here for the greatest growth period in the his-

tory of our program. He was here when we went from being an individual RoboDawgs team and an individual LEGO League team to being a program. He was the one who took our manifesto and said, "It seems like this could work," and put the resources of the school district behind us. More recently, Roger Bearup came to Grandville and has, again, lifted our program up to yet another level of involvement and success. A superintendent is critical to the success of your program. At any time we have helped other people start robotics programs, we have always helped them engage with the superintendent and get the support of their school district before they went any further.

Once you have this inventory of the five resource areas listed above completed, you can begin to look at robotics programs and determine which one, or ones, are the best fit for you as a starting point. As you decide what type of robotics teams to start, there are many such programs to consider. Grandville has had experience with nine different robotics programs, and each is unique in some ways.

If you have elementary-age students and you want to engage them in an exploration of science and robotics, *FIRST* LEGO League is a great place to start. *FIRST* LEGO League teams are composed of 10 students from fourth through sixth grades. They compete with a robot on a competition table, and complete a research project as part of their team activities. LEGO League teams run a short season, starting when school starts and normally wrapping up by the first week of December. That makes *FIRST* LEGO League an easy commitment for parents who are new to coaching. Many programs that start by focusing on an elementary group begin with the *FIRST* LEGO League.

Another robotics program built for elementary students is VEX IQ. VEX IQ is one of the newest elementary robotics programs, and they have an outstanding hardware set. VEX IQ runs a longer season than LEGO League and plays with smaller teams. The typical VEX IQ team has four or five students on it, and the season runs from early fall through February in most school districts. The VEX IQ robot is the most capable device available for elementary students. It has a built-in six-axis gyro/accelerometer that allows students to work with external devices, allows students to measure external distances and optical touch, and uses color sensors. VEX IQ is also different in that the events feature both fully autonomous and driver-controlled competition. Most VEX IQ teams compete in a weekly league for four to six weeks, and then compete in three or four full-day tournaments. VEX IQ teams can advance from local tournaments to a State Championship, and then from there onto the World Championship.

At middle school level, you could choose to run a VEX IQ team. Some middle schools that do not have elementary programs start their middle school programs with VEX IQ. This hardware is challenging for a middle school student, and if they have not already worked with it for a few years, it is an excellent start in middle school. We do not recommend starting VEX IQ in a middle school where you already have elementary teams playing. If an elementary team has used a VEX IQ robot in fourth through sixth grades, they rarely will stay interested in using that same robot system in seventh and eighth grades. But VEX IQ does present a good oppor-tunity for middle schools in school districts where there are no existing robotics programs. It is highly organized, and there are a large number of qualified event partners in most areas of the country to support you.

Another choice for middle school students is to compete in the VEX Robotics Competition. This is the largest and fastest-growing middle school and high school robotics program globally, with more than 20,000 teams from 50 countries playing in over 1,700 competitions worldwide. Many middle schools will field 4 to 10 teams. Teams build with modifiable standard parts from VEX Robotics and the V5 control system. Each team fields a robot that must start in the volume of an 18-inch cube. Teams in VRC compete as part of a two-team alliance playing against another two-team alliance on a 12'x12' field. Each match consists of a required autonomous period and a driver-controlled period. This competition structure makes it easy to incorporate autonomous programming in your program right from the beginning. We have found that the VRC program is the most successful way to introduce a new school district to middle school robotics.

At high school level, the VEX Robotic Competition is an excellent program. In many schools, parents begin by starting high school teams. If that is your desire, the VEX Robotic Competition is probably the best place for you to start. High school VEX Robotics teams typically have three to five members and they play with the same V5 system that a middle school would play with. Many schools begin with high school VRC and then add middle school VRC teams once the high school has had a few years of experience.

"We believe the biggest difficulty is in getting started," said Dan Mantz of the VEX-affiliated REC Foundation. "We have resources for teams and for coaches. Our learning curve is low, but there's still an intimidation factor. We have a new program to match new coaches and team with established ones for assistance."

At the high school level, you can also begin with Underwater Rovers. The RoboDawgs have fielded Square One Underwater Rover teams in Michigan, for example. There are also excellent programs from MATE Robotics. Underwater Rovers present a real challenge to a high school team, and it is rarely the first type of team a school district starts. Beyond basic programming and simple drive functions that a land-based robot would have, Underwater Rovers have unique design-building programming challenges. Buoyancy is a fun concept that does not come into play with land-based robots. Underwater robots can move in three-dimensions to add an additional programming challenge. Navigation and autonomous operation are more challenging when visibility is limited and you can't immediately get a fix on your exact location. Underwater Rovers are also impacted by water currents. Finally, the construction of Underwater Rovers is more challenging because many portions of the robot must be watertight. The Grandville students have really enjoyed Underwater Rovers and find them to be an important part of a complete program but, because of their advanced technologies, new teams shouldn't start with them.

Another high school competition that's very interesting is Bell Advanced Vertical Robotics. This is the most advanced aerial-drone event available to high school students. It involves building, programming, and flying multiple air and land-based robots in a 30'x20'x20'-foot cage. Students learn how software manages the flight of aerial drones. They program a drone to a complete multiple game challenges with full autonomy. The RoboDawgs have found that the building of aerial drones is challenging for most students because you are constructing something which must be balanced and remain in the air. Failure with a aerial drone is a much more challenging thing to recover from than failure with a land-based robot. Eventually, every advanced school district will have aerial-robotics teams, but they're not the place to start for a new team just getting their feet on the ground.

Another exciting place to start your robotics program would be with Botball. Botball Robotics engages middle-and high school students and team-oriented robotics competitions, and is more advanced than some of the other middle school programs that we have participated in. It's not a good first program for a new middle school, but high schools could begin with a Botball program. Botball is challenging because it requires completely autonomous robotics play. Students learn to program the robots in advance using C, C++, or Java, and the robots compete on a defined playing field. Kids use a Botball game kit, which provides all the parts and pieces you need to build your working robot. Botball also has outstanding teacher and mentor support, including training that is more evolved than on some of the other high school robotics programs. The RoboDawgs played Botball for a few years and really enjoyed the completely autonomous nature of the robot. They also preferred the fairly advanced challenges because these robots require more complicated designing and building than you would see in the VEX Robotics Competition or with BEST Robotics. Botball is a good place for a new program to start if the team has adult mentors with solid programming experience who are willing to commit significant time to travel to competitions. Botball is not common in all states in the country, and teams play a limited number of times at events that require longer distance travel than you would find in other middle school or high school robotics programs.

We would be remiss if we didn't talk about starting out your high school program with a *FIRST* Robotics Competition program. Grandville has had FRC teams for 25 years and our program started with just one FRC team in 1998. The RoboDawgs were among the earliest competitive programs in the U.S., and have grown that program now to include three high school FRC Teams. The FRC season is short. It runs from January through April, and teams design and build large custom robots to compete in an annual challenge. *FIRST* provides unique opportunities for students to work as part of a large team to create and maintain complex competitive robots. Students need to understand operator interfaces, robot mobility, locomotion, manipulators, programming, and sensors. *FIRST* Robotics teams require a large and experienced mentor base, and substantial financial resources. It is not uncommon for a *FIRST* Robotics team budget to exceed $30,000 in their first year. The RoboDawgs' three *FIRST* Robotics teams each cost approximately $50,000 a year, with the total investment each year being about $150,000. It's a worthwhile investment. It's hard to imagine a well-developed high school robotics program that did not field a *FIRST* Robotics team. But it's often better seen as an addition to an already successful high school program.

As you can see, there are lots of places you could begin your robotics program. There are multiple entry points for elementary teams, for middle school teams, and for high school teams. It's not a good idea, though, for a program to try to introduce robotics at all three academic levels in their first year.

This chapter has covered many of the things you should

understand before you jump in and start a robotics team. It has also given an outline of some of the characteristics of the key robotics programs in the U.S. What remains to be discussed is the sequence of actually starting a team. While the scope of this book is not intended to cover every aspect of starting a team, a good general summary is an outline of the six key steps in getting started. One final note before we get into the sequence. For a startup, many schools begin with one type of robotics program and field multiple teams in their first year. It would be unusual to start multiple competitive programs in the first year – trying, for instance, to start an FRC team in the high school, VRC teams in the middle school, and LEGO League teams at the elementary school all in your first year. It is very common for school districts to focus on one age group – either elementary, middle school, or high school – and for that age group to identify one type of competition: VEX Robotics competition, *FIRST* Robotics Competition, LEGO League, Bell aerial drones, or another type of competition. By focusing in these ways, new programs are most likely to be successful by starting with one type of team in one age group their first year.

If you're ready to move forward and start a team, here are the six questions you have to answer as you begin.

The first question is: Why?

You need to understand why you are starting this program. Are you starting it so three parents can have a team for their students to compete on? Are you starting it with the idea that you'll create opportunities for kids across multiple teams in your district? Are you starting a team with the idea that your middle school kids would play VRC in seventh and eighth grades and then you'd move on and broaden your program to support them in their high school years? It's very important to understand why you're doing something because this is what will keep you on track over the first year and the years that follow. Perhaps the most important part of the success in Grandville is the program's knowing its *Why*. It excites, inspires, and educates kids to explore hands-on science. It improves their academic performance. It teaches them about hands-on applications of science and technology, and how to operate as a team in the spirit of gracious professionalism. These *Whys* are important themes that run through everything the RoboDawgs do in Grandville.

After you've figured out your *Why*, next figure out *Who*.

Who's going to help provide overall leadership to your teams? Who's going to coach individual teams? Who's going to support those coaches by building fields and supporting the team as it travels? Who's going to drive fundraising for the teams and make sure there's adequate money in place to support all the teams' needs? These are all questions it's critical that you answer.

It's crucial, too, that the overall program leaders keep very tight reins on every team in the system. As with the RoboDawgs manifesto, your program should work from a specific set of guiding principles that are universal throughout the program, and all the team need to be working from that same playbook. Make sure that everyone in your program understands that and is on board with it, and that there are ways to enforce it. During some of the difficult days in the RoboDawgs' history, several coaches tried to take their teams in a different direction from the rest and, eventually, that required extreme measures to resolve – including trademarking the RoboDawgs name so that nobody else could call their teams by that name without being aligned with the central program.

Sadly, sometimes you will have to "fire" a coach too. Not everyone is cut out for the demands that robotics coaches have to face and deal with, just as not everyone is suited to particular jobs in the working world. When you have a mismatch that's hurting the teams, you must have procedures in place to remove the person who's failing to perform from the situation. As difficult as it might be, it's important to face that reality before you're confronted with it, and to know beforehand how your program will handle the situation.

Once you've answered the *Why* and the *Who*, now it's time for *What?*

What ages are your teams going to support? What type of teams are you going to start? How many teams are you going to start? *What* is where your *Why* and *Who* turns into exactly what you are going to do in your first year. While it's important to have a vision beyond the first year, it's important to get the *What* right in your very first months.

The next question is: Where?

Your students need a place to design, build, program, and test their robots. They probably need a place to set up a field and practice. They need a place that's open at the hours that you want to build, practice, and compete. This is where your public school, church, or corporate sponsor comes into play. You need an organization with a facility that will support your aspirations. Unless you're going to want a single team with six kids in your basement, you're going to need a place where multiple teams can practice, build, and compete. The space requirements are very different for different programs. LEGO League plays on a 4'x8' field that can be set on top of anybody's table. VEX IQ plays on a 6'x8' plastic field that can be set up on any floor in any room. The VEX Robotics Competition, however, requires a 12'x12' field that can be complex to assemble, which you won't want to put up and take down every week. If you're going to play *FIRST* Robotics, the *FIRST* Robotics field is 27'x54', and it takes several weeks to build a field. Once you know the *Who* and the *What* for your program, answer the *Where* and make sure you have the right space to support your teams.

Now it's time to contemplate your *When?*

You know what teams you want to run and who's going to run them, but when are you going to run your teams? Are you going to start your season in the first week of September or on the first day of October? Are you going to try to extend your season to allow your teams to continue to build and program to attend a national championship that might occur in April? Are you going to attempt to run a program just for one season or the whole school year? Defining your overall season is important as you begin to commit kids and adults to competing in your first year. Within the season, there are also questions to be answered. How many hours a week are you going to practice, and for how long each time? It is very hard to have elementary school students practice for three hours at a time. Their attention span and their willingness to stay focused, or their ability to stay focused, does not extend for three hours. It is common for elementary LEGO League teams to practice for an hour, or an hour and a half, twice a week. It is common for middle school teams to practice for longer at a time, and more frequently. It is not uncommon to see a VEX Robotics Competition team at middle school level practice two or three times a week for two hours at a time. Determine for each team how long each practice will run, and how many times a week you want to practice.

Now look at competing. Once you've defined your practice time, do you want to compete in a weekly league, committing two to four hours a week to compete with other robots? Do you want to compete in full-day tournaments once a month or twice a month? Do you want to compete five or six times during the year, or 10 times? Do you intend to compete at state or national levels? All these decisions about where you want to compete will have implications for when you are going to meet with your team and how much time this is going to take. It's important to understand those things early on.

Finally, the last question: How?

Now it's time to put together your plan to actually get going. This plan needs to lay out how you're going to promote your teams to students, and how you're going to sign them up. There are many details about starting up. This leads to our final topic for this chapter of starting teams – one of the most important things to think about as you start.

Mike and Doug's experience starting teams across multiple school districts, in multiple states and countries, has led them to conclude there are three more things that are really important to understand when you commit to a robotics team.

The first is you need to find a friend. No adult should ever take on a robotics team or program by themselves. You always need at least a couple of committed adults, a couple of friends, who will bring the band together. Those two friends or three friends need to look across their group of interested adults and form the core group that will drive your team. Frequently, that is a husband and a wife who have two other couples that want to support them. Sometimes it's a teacher and a parent who decide to coach a team and then have parents support that team. If you're going to have multiple teams, you're going to need a couple of friends to run the program, and then a process to recruit, train, and support parents who will coach the additional teams. Finding a friend is the most important thing you'll do to assure the success of your program.

You'll find that, to create a consistent, long-term program, it takes those two or three people at the top, especially if you want a program that covers elementary, middle, and high schools. Ideally, those coaches will have very different backgrounds and perspectives, as that's how you get leadership that works across the broad spectrum of people and activities that are involved in a successful robotics program. And eventually, you'll also need a whole host of other adult volunteers, and some of them should be willing to stick with the program even after their own kids have graduated. A successful school robotics program is bigger than one person or the sum of its parts. There have to be torchbearers – one or two or three adult leaders who go beyond the basics of coaching and become champions for the program over the long haul.

> **Doug:** Running a robotics program is tough and, while it's a lot of fun and there are tremendous results, it's not something that anyone takes on for 365 days a year without sometimes feeling the weight of the program. Every year, you reach the point where you say, "I may have had enough of this." That second torchbearer is so helpful because you do end up going to them and saying, "I don't know about this," and they remind you of all the things that are valuable, of all the success-

es you've had, of the impact you have, and of all the reasons you do this. That second torchbearer brings you back on board, and you go forward together again. Having someone along is really important.

Mike: Yes, there is one night every year where one of us goes for a walk and says to himself, "I'm done. I'm quitting, this is too much," and usually ends up walking to the other guy's house, and somehow, we support each other and we get through it, solve our problems, and move on. But every year, there's the March walk.

Once you find a friend, now build your group of adult leaders. Depending on the age of your students and the type of program you're running, you are going to need between 4 and 20 coaches to help you. Most likely, you don't have a group of adults that know that right now. You're going to have to figure that out.

Finally, before you start a robotics program, find another program to help you. There are existing event partners and teams operating in schools all around you. If there are students' teams operating somewhere in the U.S., that would help you. It is very important to have an experienced guide at your side as you start to build your first teams and get started with your program. The RoboDawgs, for example, have helped people start teams across nine different types of robotics competitions, across multiple states of the U.S., and across multiple provinces in Canada.

The RoboDawgs have found it is exciting to help new programs because their experience can help others avoid many of the mistakes they had to learn their own way through. They have found that they can help new teams structure themselves and start their recruiting process. The RoboDawgs have made their parts inventories available to new teams as well, lending them equipment to get them started. They've used their own training programs to help other teams train new coaches. They've also found that their events can give new teams a place to play in their early years.

To reiterate, if you're going to start a robotics team, you need to find a friend. You need to enlist the help of multiple adult leaders, and you should find an existing program to help you start more easily down the path.

THE FUTURE OF COMPETITIVE ROBOTICS AND THE GRANDVILLE ROBODAWGS

Even though competitive robotics has been around for over three decades now, it's still actively carving out its purpose – even while it constantly adapts to the insane pace of changes in technology.

The central concept that Dean Kamen came up with back at the end of the 1980s remains in place – the belief that competitive robotics will attract more students to STEM fields and expand the highly skilled workforce that the increasing demands of technology place on our society. If anything, that purpose has expanded. Academic robotics now reaches almost every level of pre-secondary education, and the technologies involved have grown dramatically. When you consider the fact that, when FRC began in 1989, pretty much nobody had cell phones or personal computers, you get a sense for how much technology has changed – and how it has changed *us* – in the intervening years.

Educational robotics has come a long way during that time. To understand where it's headed, it's important to understand the reasons it has evolved at an increasing pace.

The evolution of competitive robotics has been driven by three factors: 1) robotics programs have grown based on enhanced sources of funding; 2) changes to the organizing principles of the sponsoring entities have further driven growth; 3)advancements in technology and education have broadened the offerings of these programs.

They say if you want to understand something, you should follow the money. If you look at competitive educational robotics, all the early money flowed from a single organizing program and corporate sponsors. As noted in earlier chapters of the book, *FIRST* Robotics really started everything. Their introduction of the *FIRST* Robotics Competition in 1992 started the evolution of competitive robotics. At that time, money came from *FIRST* themselves and from corporate sponsors. There was limited local and no state support for competitive robotics. Over the years, this funding model has changed, and that has made a tremendous difference in the evolution of these programs. We have moved from program-specific funding that was available in the earlier years to public funding on a much broader scale. *FIRST* Robotics has always provided funding to build more *FIRST* teams, and there have been tremendous financial incentives to move from high school FRC into elementary LEGO League.

Just as the bulk of funding available ten years ago for such programs came from *FIRST* Robotics and their sponsors, the same was true of the RECF and VEX Robotics. A decade ago, as VEX was growing, most of the funding to start new VEX teams came through VEX grants from the RECF. This model has changed. Today, there is substantial state and local funding for robotics programs, which has allowed us to expand into more, and different, types of robotics and to develop additional teams. In the state of Michigan, the legislature approved Section 99h of the Michigan Education Department's Annual Budget. This grant program provides funding for all types of competitive robotics in public schools. It provides thousands of dollars to every local school district to support the development and maintenance of competitive robotics teams. The 99h program provides funding for parts and fields, as well as program registration fees. It also is unique in that it provides funding to support mentors, providing up to $1,500 a year for a mentor of a robotics team. Local support has also grown.

Ten years ago, it would be unheard of for a school district in Michigan to provide dedicated space and funding to multiple robotics teams at multiple educational levels. This has changed dramatically, and today, it is not uncommon for a school district to provide dedicated space for high school teams. It is also not unusual for a district to provide, from their annual budget, funding to support teams at elementary, middle school, and high school levels. This commitment varies largely across programs, but it is dramatically different to what it was a decade ago. This shift in funding, from funding driven by national sponsoring entities to funding driven by state and local entities, has driven an explosion in the number and type of competitive robotic teams. A district that might have had only an FRC team 10 years ago now likely has VEX IQ or LEGO League teams. It may have an Underwater Rover team, and it may have an aerial-robotics team. This shift in funding away from funding dependent on a national entity that sponsors robotics programs has allowed for the evolution of many new programs.

The second factor impacting the evolution of competitive robotics teams is the organizing principles of the sponsoring entity. *FIRST* Robotics was first. When they began, there was nothing to work from. *FIRST* Robotics, by design, had a very top-down structure where rules were set and policies established, and they were pushed down from a national organization to a state organization to a local team. This structure was necessary in the early years of competitive robotics, as there was no existing infrastructure. *FIRST* continues to have this type of structure today, which both makes it strong and limits its growth. The RECF and VEX Robotics took a different approach. The RECF is an umbrella organization, which invests in and relies tremendously on the local event partner. The RECF works as an organizing entity, taking the best ideas from local event partners and taking advice from advisory councils to create a set of national policies driven more by consensus than a top-down decision-making process. This fundamental difference in the RECF has allowed them to grow much more rapidly and become the dominant organizer of competitive robotics teams for schools in North America. The RECF started with VEX Robotics and, over the years, added VEX IQ for elementary students. They added the aerial-drone competition, and they added Bell Advanced Vertical Robotics. The organizing principles behind the RECF are very democratically inspired and are built around the principle that the most important people in the ecosystem are their event partners. This has yielded an organization which innovates quickly and grows rapidly. It enforces uniformity in refereeing and judging, while still providing local organizations room to evolve in ways that are most appropriate in their schools.

A third factor impacting the evolution of educational robotics are the changes in technology and education itself. When the RoboDawgs began, they used one set of technology, provided by *FIRST* Robotics. It was a standard set of electronics, which was used by every team in the country. It was expensive and, at the time, fairly leading-edge. A quarter-century later, technology has evolved tremendously. An example is the aerial-drone programs in Grandville Public Schools. The RoboDawgs built their first drones in 2013, and each drone cost about $8,000. These drones had limited capabilities. They had either four or eight motors and rotors, a flight controller, a GPS, and a power-distribution board. These drones could maintain flight and could navigate from point to point using basic GPS coordinates. These drones had limited ability to operate in windy conditions, and collision avoidance was not practical given the state of onboard computing at that time. Today, the RoboDawgs compete in the Bell Advanced Vertical Robotics Competition. The Bell drone that the teams compete with each year requires approximately $2,500 in parts. This drone, like its predecessors, has four rotors and motors, a power-distribution board, and a flight controller. That's where the similarities end. Today's drones also carry multiple onboard processors, multiple onboard cameras, vision-processing systems, and an event manager which manages the inputs from all the various devices and allows the drone to make decisions autonomously about what to do. These drones are highly stable in windy conditions and have significant collision-avoidance capabilities. The technology of drones, moving from an $8,000 drone in 2013 to a $2,500 drone in 2023, provides capabilities that are several orders of magnitude greater now than they had in the early years.

This advancement in technology also comes through in ground-based robots. Today's VEX robots compete in VEX AI, and play a fully autonomous two-and-a-half-minute game. There is no driver control – no joystick. This form of competition would have been impractical even five years ago given the cost and capability of technology available at the time. Today's VEX AI robots also carry multiple processors and a full range of sensors, including distance, touch, and 3D gyros. They carry highly capable camera systems, which track multiple targets and can provide the robot with not only the location of each target in X and Y coordinates, but also the distance from the robot to each of the targets. This type of sensing and processing power was unavailable at a school competitive level five years ago. The evolution of technology like this will continue to redefine what educational robotics looks like.

Advances in education have also changed competitive robotics. Over the last 10 years, we have seen a significant increase in the number of computer-science courses taught at the high school and middle school levels. We have seen a dramatic increase in project-based learning providing hands-on technology training in classrooms. We have also seen the rebirth of technical education in our high schools. High schools that had largely done away with "shop" classes have re-engaged in the technical-education area. It is common now for high schools to have metal shops, CNC machines, and 3D printers. This re-engagement with technical education has had a significant impact on the ability of schools to produce graduates who are ready for a career, not only in college, but also in a trade. It has also supported the development of competitive robotics teams, as these skills are critical to the fabrication of competitive robots.

Over the last ten years, competitive robotics has also seen the development of new programs that are more accessible to a larger group of schools. In the early days, *FIRST*

Robotics was only accessible to a school that had substantial corporate sponsorship. *FIRST* Robotics teams require substantial financial resources and a deep mentor base. That puts FRC teams out of reach for many public schools. When Bob and Tony started VEX Robotics, one of their stated objectives was to create a program that was more accessible and provided more equitable opportunities for kids to work with technology. VEX Robotics has been successful in that regard, as you can easily start a VEX Robotics program with one adult and limited financial funding in any school district in the U.S. There are VEX Robotics competitions in every state in the Union, and in most states, there are competitions every week throughout the competition season. The model that VEX started, designed to provide broader access and more equitable access to technology across all public schools, has had a major impact on the development of competitive robotics today and will have a major impact going forward.

Let's look at the next five years for the RoboDawgs program. Grandville has many advantages, based on its history in competitive robotics. The district has a broad range of existing donors that support their teams. They have a mentor base that numbers in the hundreds. Grandville operates the country's largest built-for-purpose competitive-robotics facility. These factors are going to drive tremendous evolution in Grandville over the next five years.

At the elementary level, the opening of the new Robotics Competition Center in Grandville has allowed the district to dedicate more than four times as much space to elementary robotics teams than it has in the past. It also provided unique space and resources to enable us to launch a new Robot Combat program for students starting in third grade.

Our elementary programs have taken over all the space

in the former alternative high school that had held all our robotics teams prior to the opening of the Robotics Competition Center. Creating more times and places to play, coupled with additional space for teams to build and practice, is enabling an elementary program that will be twice its current size within five years. The program, once again, is reaching down to second grade, and we take second-through sixth-grade students into our elementary programs. It will increasingly be involved with project-based classroom activities, carrying over the technology and organization of competitive robotics into discreet units offered in elementary classrooms to expose students to hands-on technology and programming. This expansion in the elementary ages will continue to grow the number of young girls that are exposed to, and comfortable with, computer-science and engineering principles.

At the middle school level, the Grandville program has grown beyond a focus on after-school VEX Robotics Competitions and the RECF's aerial-drone competition. Our robotics program has supported the introduction of a robotics unit in our middle school STEM classes. We are about to launch an aerial-drones unit in the middle school STEM classes. Our robotics equipment and experience has enabled us to influence the STEM curriculum at our middle school, and every middle school student is now learning to program and compete with ground or aerial robots. During our first year in the new Robotics Competition Center, we introduced Robot Combat for our middle school students. In collaboration with the local MultiGP chapter, we added a drone-racing program for middle school students. Our high school students have competed with Underwater Rovers and, looking to the future, we expect to offer Underwater Rover teams at the middle school level.

At the high school level, Grandville Public Schools has dramatically grown the scope and number of robotics competitions in the new Robotic Competition Center. The opening of the new center has allowed for much more frequent robotics competitions. We run events on multiple weekday evenings and on most Saturdays. In just one year, the space in Grandville's Robotics Competition Center has become the most utilized space in the school district. More students spend more hours in this space than in any other space in our schools. Our new space has benefitted thousands of area students who come to play here each week. It draws teams from around the region to Grandville to play, exposing Grandville teams to an increasingly strong group of competitors they can learn from. Moving into the new Robotics Competition Center has allowed Grandville to devote more time to evolving its program and less time to running events.

Over the last past five years, when Grandville wanted to run a 48-team VEX Robotics Competition event, it took two days and more than 100 volunteers. In order to run an event of this size, Grandville would reserve the high school gyms, and then move two trailers' worth of equipment into those gyms for the competition. The setup would begin after school on a Friday and extend until 10pm, with more than 50 volunteers working to set up fields, sound systems, video systems, queuing areas, and support areas, such as a cafeteria and judging rooms. In the new facility, Grandville leaves everything in place to run a 48-team throughout the VEX season. It is now possible, because of the space that's dedicated, to turn on the lights and host a 48-team VEX Robotics Competition event with a half-hour of preparation.

The new facility has four permanent fields for VEX Robotics Competitions, as well as six more practice and skills fields. It has dedicated sound and video in place to support audience displays and live webcasts. We have a cafeteria on site, and a dedicated concession area. This ability to host events with no setup or tear-down time has put Grandville in a position to host VEX Robotics events on multiple days of the week. It is now common for us to run a 24-team VEX V5 or VEX IQ league night multiple times a week.

Not only does the new facility benefit VEX Robotics, it has also opened up time and space for a full high school FRC field, drone racing, and all our elementary and middle school competitions. Again, having the space to leave fields and practice areas set up throughout the school year has allowed Grandville to take all the time that was devoted to setting up and running competitions and put that time into developing and coaching new programs. Grandville has been through a tremendous evolution over the last 25 years. The district grew its program from one *FIRST* Robotics team to more than 100 teams playing in ground, underwater, and air competitions. It has grown from a team that was funded by one corporate sponsor to more than 100 teams that are sponsored by dozens of companies and families – as well as the team's program handling returnable bottles and cans.

It's amazing how one little thing can have such a profound impact on a program. The Grandville robotics programs began collecting bottles and cans for the Michigan deposit during the COVID-19 period. What started out as something to make a little money during the lean years of the COVID restrictions has turned into an effort which provides a third of the team's funding. Grandville robotics teams return more than 1.5 million cans and bottles each year, turning those returnables into $150,000 in cash to support our programs. Who would have thought 25 years ago that returnable cans and bottles would play a big role in Grandville's competitive robotics program?

The Grandville robotics program is fairly unique. Its leaders have strived over the years to defend two principles, and the tremendous support they receive from area families, companies, and the public has allowed them to stay this course.

First, our programs are not pay-to-play. Grandville does not believe that a student's opportunity to participate in a robotics team should be defined by their family's ability to write a big check. Other area robotics teams charge students up to $2,800 a year, plus travel expenses, to participate on a robotics team. None of Grandville Public Schools' competitive robotic programs have been pay-to-play at any point in their 27-year history. It is the belief of Grandville leadership that this is a key feature of our programs.

Second, Grandville builds world-caliber teams because they try to make room for every student who wants to participate. From second grade through graduation, they create opportunities for all students who want to create and compete. This is almost unheard of in the world of competitive educational robotics, and many programs accept less than 30% of the students that apply. Grandville's policy has been to accept all students who can comply with the program's academic and behavioral requirements to participate at no charge to the family.

It will be exciting to see where the Grandville RoboDawgs go. Grandville has been a supporter and developer of competitive robotics teams in other school districts all over North America, and where Grandville goes, so shall hundreds of other school districts. Here's to the future – technology will continue to race forward, education will continue to evolve, and our society will continue to increase its support of competitive programs where every student can go pro.

ABOUT THE AUTHORS

Michael Evele has been a physics teacher for 36 years and counting. He was a Science Olympiad coach for 21 years (including student teaching). In 1998, he, along with Natalie Lowell and Spencer Dolloff, founded the RoboDawgs. Though teaching physics is his passion, as with most teachers, it's really all about the students. Mike is grateful for an amazing career getting to know and love so many incredible students.

Doug Hepfer was a successful partner at one of the world's largest consulting firms and currently runs his own firm. He discovered competitive robotics when he and his wife Rosemary volunteered to coach his son's elementary LEGO League team. That one team turned into two, then four, and then more than 20 LEGO League teams in Grandville, Michigan. Doug had been a church youth group leader, a mission trip organizer, and a scoutmaster – but he found he had a passion for the way competitive robotics altered the trajectories of the kids that participated.

Jim Vinoski is president of Cosgrove Content and Consulting, an advisory and multimedia content creation firm focused on storytelling in manufacturing. With over 35 years of industry experience at such companies as Ralston Purina and General Mills, he is a manufacturing contributor for Forbes and host of the Manufacturing Talks Web Show and Podcast. After featuring the RoboDawgs in a Forbes article about the workforce development aspects of competitive robotics, Jim signed on to help Doug and Mike tell their remarkable story.

www.CompetitiveRoboticsPress.com

ACKNOWLEDGMENTS

This book tells the story of the RoboDawgs and the impact that this competitive robotics program has had on our students, schools, community, and businesses. It is a twenty-six year success story, which would not have been possible without the contributions made by hundreds of important parents, educators, and sponsors. It would be impossible to list all those who have made a meaningful contribution to this program, and we thank everyone who has supported the Grandville robotics programs in some way. We give a shout-out to the following people who have had a major impact on the program.

Duane Sheldon
Roger Bearup
Scott Merkel
Natalie Lowell
Ron Denning
Scott Joseph
Jeff Nelson
Bill and Carol Welch
Ann and Chris Leaver
Bill Pokora
Joelle Snidanko
Morrie Cunningham

Ron Caniff
Chris VanderSlice
Adam Lancto
Larry Lowell
Spencer Dolloff
Ken Orzechowski
Dan Hall
Bob Wondergem
Aivars Apsite
Frank Spica
Tim and Donna Bos
Doug Howerzyl

George and Kelly Nichols
Mike Hepfer
Amy and Dave Furman
Karen and Ray Cheydleur
Grason Cheydleur
Al and Melanie Fischer
Tori Buck
Bill and Karen LaBarge
Gasper and Dara
Rick Veldheer
Jason and Brenda Bargenquast
Heather and Chris Buckler
Patrick Johnson
Chris Callahan
Stacy Petersen
Kim and Mike Slager
Scott and April Hammond
Jason and Rachael O'Callaghan

Art and Jenelle Danner
Thomas Bos
Peggy Monroe
Chuck Parks
Dan Mantz
Greg Simonte
Brian Courtade
Kelly Herb
Amy Hiller
Greg Wilson
Steve Licata
Jennifer Swieringa
Kin Ma
Radka Mateju
Christine Sikora
Kevin Still
Chuck Aman
Zack Veldheer

.